layout workbook

ROCKPORT

a real-world guide to
building pages in graphic design

LAYOUT
WORKBOOK

KRISTIN CULLEN

ROCKPORT PUBLISHERS

First published in the United States of America by Rockport Publishers, Inc.

33 Commercial Street
Gloucester, Massachusetts 01930–5089
978.282.9590 *p*
978.283.2742 *f*
www.rockpub.com

Library of Congress Cataloging-in-Publication Data
Cullen, Kristin.
    Layout workbook: a real-world guide to building pages in graphic design /
written and designed by Kristin Cullen.
        p.   cm.
    ISBN 1–59253–158–X (hc)

    1. Graphic arts—Technique. 2. Graphic design (Typography)
3. Advertising layout and typography. I. Title.

    NC1000.C85 2005
    741.6--dc22

                                                                    2004026252
                                                                    CIP

ISBN 1–59253–158–X
10 9 8 7 6 5 4 3 2

Layout and cover design: Kristin Cullen

Printed in China

To design is
to transform prose into poetry.

PAUL RAND
author, graphic designer, teacher

Art is not what you see,
but what
you make others see.

EDGAR DEGAS
painter, sculptor

Design is the visual synthesis of ideas. It captures thought and
language, transforming them anew. Design also commands the
imagination and intellect, creates connections, fosters understanding, and provides meaning. Compelling examples of visual
communication solutions range from simple to complex, trivial
to significant. Design shapes the visible environment and delivers
information to everyone within it; it is functional, conveying messages with purpose. Design is always present, taking on myriad
formats, including print, digital, and environmental. Engrained
into the fabric of cultural experience, design affects daily life
in mundane and extraordinary ways.

For the designer, design is a creative journey—a process of discovery—that is fueled by inspiration and creative passion, as well as the desire to enrich and ignite communication. Designers are the engineers and craftsman of visual messages. They contribute their learned and innate knowledge, critical thinking and analysis abilities, and acute aesthetic and visual skills to the process. Design is an intriguing, evolutionary field, and the designer must constantly adapt to satisfy and challenge the ever-changing needs of communication.

Although design and designers continue to advance and diversify, the basic foundation of design practice lies in the understanding and application of the fundamentals of layout. The following pages are dedicated to these fundamentals, examining the function and importance of visual communication. The book illuminates the broad category of layout from function, inspiration, process, and intuition to structure, hierarchy, and typography. The objective is to educate and inspire as well as promote creativity, while encouraging the design of strong, thoughtful, and informative layouts. Featuring primarily print communications, each chapter aims to engage the viewer emotionally, intellectually, and visually—sharing the wonder of design.

THE **FUNCTION**

To design
 is much more than
 simply to assemble, to order, or even to edit; it is
 to add value and meaning,
 to illuminate, to simplify, to clarify,
 to modify, to dignify,
 to dramatize, to persuade,
 and perhaps even
 to amuse.

PAUL RAND
author, graphic designer, teacher

OF **DESIGN**

The function of graphic design is the communication of messages through the juxtaposition of words and pictures. It is the visual synthesis of thought in the form of publications, exhibitions, and posters, as well as packaging, signage, and digital interfaces. Design is tactile, environmental, and interactive. Responding to public needs, it is a powerful visual medium that is present in all aspects of daily life. Graphic design extends itself into cultural experiences and speaks to society on practical, emotional, and intuitive levels. It affects human experience from the most mundane to the most extraordinary ways.

design objectives

communication

education

information

guidance

encouragement

promotion

inspiration

awareness

dialogue

persuasion

entertainment

direction

motivation

Directed toward individuals and groups, design delivers information to intended recipients who receive and use (or ignore and abandon) it in countless ways. The function of design is not decoration. Though sophisticated aesthetics and excellent visual execution are essential to the design, communicative function is absolutely imperative—it is the primary purpose. Design educates, inspires, and entertains, as well as informs and encourages. Design also creates awareness and nurtures dialogue, while directing, guiding, motivating, promoting, and persuading. It conveys and ignites attitudes and emotions. Design is remarkably multifunctional.

| *design* lichtwitz | Packaging establishes the mood of the product that lies inside. It is the first impression of the piece and dramatically influences its marketability.

| *design* greteman group |
Posters must create immediate visual impact with strong focal points that direct the eye into the composition and lead the viewer toward subordinate content that is accessible upon closer examination.

| *design* wilsonharvey/loewy |
Business cards are components of a larger identity system and represent people, businesses, and organizations. They serve as reminders or symbols of an exchange, dialogue, or meeting, yet also have a practical function and must convey the essential contact details clearly.

establishing function

The function of the design must be established before the design process can begin.

Is the design an invitation, annual report, poster, or book?
What is its primary objective?
Who is it trying to reach?
What is the desired reaction of the viewer?

Determining the function of the piece is critical and provokes numerous questions that inform the designer and help focus the development of the design.

determining the function of the design

Will the design...

announce or invite and request participation?

inform and create awareness?

educate or instruct?

identify or symbolize and represent people, places, and things?

illustrate and explain?

spark imagination and ignite creativity?

interpret and clarify?

influence and motivate action?

solicit trust or faith?

package, promote, sell, or advertise?

protect and store?

guide and provide navigation?

display and exhibit?

commemorate and mark history?

feature and showcase?

anger and incite?

entertain and amuse?

| *design* rmac | *Invitations promote and request participation. They are timely; once the event ends, the design no longer serves its primary task.*

| *design* visual dialogue | *Design creates awareness and motivates action. It can inspire individuals to open their minds, while actively participating in events that bring positive change to local, national, and global communities.*

the role of the designer

The designer adopts multiple personalities throughout the design process. They are analysts, strategists, decision makers, and managers, as well as articulate problem solvers and conceptual and symbolic thinkers. The designer often plays the roles of writer and editor, as well as cultural anthropologist and sociologist. They must possess a broad range of skills to effectively solve visual communication problems with impact. The designer must understand the relationship between color, form, and space, as well as structure, hierarchy, and typography. Through education and practice, the designer builds their skills, while enhancing intellect and visual acuity. It is the designer's primary responsibility to create strong communicative experiences that support the function of the design on behalf of the client and for the viewer.

the skills of the designer

problem solving

communication

analysis

visualization

management

composition

organization

information-gathering

systemization

critical thinking

aesthetics

representation

research

perception

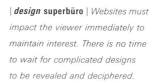

| *design* cave images | Announcements share, entertain, inform, and celebrate. They can be playful or serious, dry or witty, simple or ornate.

| *design* no.parking | Books entertain and educate for extended periods of time. They require in-depth engagement, so the layout must be consistent, dynamic, and readable to maintain attention.

| *design* superbüro | Websites must impact the viewer immediately to maintain interest. There is no time to wait for complicated designs to be revealed and deciphered.

The designer simplifies, translates, and shares ideas through the thoughtfully and carefully executed manipulation of the visual elements. The appropriate relationship of form to content, as well as the utility and function of the design, is managed by the designer. The designer develops and controls the visual presentation of information to enable comprehension and relate form to function with aesthetic grace; they create meaning and send messages through visualization. The designer must communicate information in an accessible and effective visual format that serves the function of the design, not the designer.

FINAL THOUGHTS The primary function of design is the communication of messages. Ideas are shared from person to person through compelling visualization. It is a challenge to effectively deliver messages that are dynamic, engaging, and informative, while satisfying the objectives of everyone participating and affected by the design process and final visual solution. The designer plays a pivotal role, shaping visual communication to create connections between the client and viewer.

| *design* mitre design | *Design commemorates history. It succinctly captures the essence of the past, brings it into the present, and carries its memory into the future.*

| *design* creative inc. | *Branding creates a unified identity and visual image that can be applied to multiple pieces. Well-planned and clearly articulated guidelines help others understand and follow the strategic system.*

I begin with an idea,

and then it becomes something else.

PABLO PICASSO

artist, ceramist, painter, printmaker, sculptor

INSPIRATION

CULTIVATING CREATIVITY

Inspiration is boundless. From places and books to culture and art, as well as nature and science, inspiration comes from everywhere, and the opportunities for seeking it are without end. Inspiration is the spirit or energy that motivates the creative process and provides the impetus to solve communication problems. It engages the senses of the designer and fosters originality. Inspiration signals the beginning of an idea. It guides and informs the designer, giving shape to visual solutions and bringing communication to life. It defines the navigable pathway that leads to clear and dynamic designs.

discovering inspiration

Inspiration is found (or discovered) and transformed into tangible objects. It cannot be defined easily as one specific thing or another because inspirational factors are different for everyone. Two designers can share the same experience, yet only one may find something special that sparks creative insights and furthers the passion for design. Inspiration arrives as a result of the unique way the designer looks at, and reacts to, his or her environment. Everyone's senses are piqued in unique ways, yet everyone has the potential to visually interpret his or her findings and make the ordinary extraordinary. From city lights to architecture to materials and textures, anything can spark ideas that will develop into concrete solutions. No matter what inspires, the influence of inspiration keeps the designer moving forward and encourages continued development toward advanced, thoughtful, and dynamic work.

Attentiveness, observation, and open-mindedness are critical to identifying inspiration, which can arrive at any time without notice. The designer must be fully aware of his or her environment, always looking for anything that commands attention or stirs emotions in positive and negative ways. Inspiration is captivating, originating from both good and bad situations. Learning to see, listen, and feel with acuteness is critical to gleaning inspiration. The designer must willingly, actively, and carefully examine everything and pay close attention to details.

| *design* rick johnson & company |

This letterhead system for Belize Saltwater Outfitters, a company specializing in fishing tours in Belize, reflects the themes of adventure and travel. Design director Tim McGrath found design inspiration in books, including Carouschka's Tickets (*pictured*), Hong Kong Apothecary: A Visual History of Chinese Medicine Packaging, *and* Maya Designs.

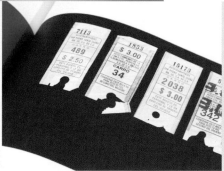

DAY WEAR

| *design* crush | The catalog for Simultané—a boutique and fashion label—was inspired by their collection as well as a designer's sketchbook. Photographs of the Simultané studio, fabric samples, sketches, and notes are incorporated into the design. The inspirational findings, which are layered throughout the piece, reflect the creative process that sparks the design of the clothing.

Seeking inspiration is not a chore that requires extra effort. Rather, it is a natural reaction that stems from the desire to create and communicate. The designer must experience life and vigorously explore the inspirational forces of daily environments, taking as much from them as possible. In addition to outside influences, the designer must also look inward and tap into the subconscious, which is another useful source of creative inspiration. In addition, recalling past experiences is equally powerful as inspirational and motivational factors that influence the design process.

THE DESIGNER MUST **WILLINGLY**, **ACTIVELY**, AND **CAREFULLY** EXAMINE EVERYTHING AND PAY CLOSE ATTENTION TO DETAILS.

| *design* d-fuse | D-Tonate_00 DVD is a progressive collection of multi-angle films and multiaudio tracks. From the cover design and interior packaging to the digital interface and films, a primary source of inspiration was Japan, which is where the piece was initially launched.

Amassing a collection of inspirational notes, drawings, photographs, quotations, and sounds (the elements of the collection are limitless) is a valuable resource for every designer. It is important to capture inspiration in any form when it strikes, even if it cannot be used immediately. In time, the inspiration will find its place and reveal its value as the beginning seed of the design process. The collection can take on any format that best suits the individual designer. It can be a notebook or sketchbook, as well as a storage box or pin-up board, which the designer adds to on a daily basis. Use the collection to create new and inventive solutions, which could become inspiration for other designers.

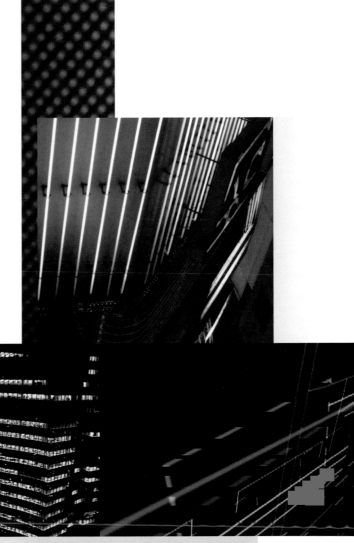

| design d-fuse | Urban architecture and lights as well as maps, graphic shapes, and textures contribute to the visual language system used throughout the design.

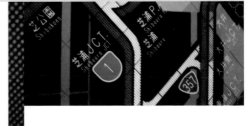

nurturing inspiration

Carry a notebook or camera everywhere to record findings.

Become immersed in design.

Be committed to discovering and collecting inspirational factors.

Take a walk.

Take breaks throughout the day.

Listen to music.

Spend the day outdoors.

Communicate regularly with other designers.

Explore areas of interest beyond design.

Go to a movie, play, opera, concert, museum, or gallery opening.

Visit family and friends.

Read design and nondesign books, magazines, and journals.

Go for a drive.

Attend conferences, lectures, and events.

Take a different route home after work.

Explore.

Create diversions from everyday routines.

Go on vacation or spend a weekend away from home.

Try something new.

Learning to develop the ability to perceive, gather, and use inspiration is the responsibility of the designer. It is important to react to the everyday environment with heightened senses, making the most of all experiences. Inspiration provides tremendous insight toward creativity and design. The wellspring of inspirational factors (and knowledge gained from them) shapes and influences the designer and the design process in countless ways. Inspiration is the first step toward the final design.

| **design** mitre design | *This poster for the Downtown Farmers Market combines a range of inspirational factors, including folk art, old advertisements, and packaging labels. The sources of inspiration are weathered, typographically bold, and richly colored; these qualities are reflected in the design. The inspiration influences the eclectic, yet contemporary, composition that features diverse, hand-crafted letterforms and a rustic color palette.*

THE DESIGN

a real-world

The recognition of
the value of the journey,
as opposed to the imagined value points of ending,
informs the idea of process.

TOMATO
london-based art collective

PROCESS

UNDERSTANDING METHODOLOGY

Design is a process of discovery. It is a journey that reveals communication through distinct stages, which include research and information-gathering, brainstorming, conceptualization, experimentation and development, and execution. When approaching any design problem, the focus of the designer must not be on the final product. Although the end result is important, the path that leads to it is equally significant. Valuable discoveries and insights, which foster growth and understanding, are gained through each stage of the design process. No matter how large or small the project, every step demands full attention. Though the design process is exhausting at times, especially if the designer is working under time restrictions, it will ultimately benefit the outcome of the design, as well as the designer.

the value of process
developing a project brief

Design is an analytical field that demands a range of skills, including management, problem solving, and visual acuity. At the beginning of the process, a great deal of planning is required before sketching and designing can begin. An intellectual methodology will guide the designer, as well as the design, from initiation to completion. The design process is the foundation on which layouts are systematically built. It is the supporting guide that allows the designer to control the progression of the project from one stage to the next.

The design process also encourages the designer to carefully scrutinize the communication problem and cultivate an effective solution. It enables the designer to understand the project and its intended function before visual studies begin. Whereas the stages of the design process remain the same with every project, the passage through the stages is uncharted. The designer must be open to altering its course to produce diverse, original, and useful visual solutions. Additionally, to avoid derivation or imitation, the designer must be careful not jump into the conceptualization, development, and execution stages too quickly or without enough background support. The design must be comprehensively considered from beginning to end to avoid naïve ideas that do not effectively solve the problem.

Preparing the project brief is an essential step that initiates the design process. As the preparatory stage, the brief provides a meticulous overview of the project, while informing all parties involved in the development and production of the design. The project brief addresses the design in detail and includes every aspect of the problem, as well as the roles of the client, designer, and viewer. It is used throughout the process as a reference tool to ensure that the design reflects the project objectives, moves in the proper direction, and relates to the needs of the client and viewer. Design must be calculated and meaningful and should reflect its function with a high degree of communicative and aesthetic proficiency.

defining the essential details The project brief
commences with a detailed review of the research and information provided by the client, which the designer needs to
clarify and simplify for efficient use. Throughout the development of the brief, questions should address initial and
long-term concerns, as well as responsibilities and expectations. The designer is not expected to know everything, but
he or she is responsible for asking the client to fill in any
missing pieces. Additionally, the designer should never make
decisions based on assumptions; collaboration with the client
is absolutely critical. There is no excuse for confusion or mis-
understandings at any stage of the process. All details should
be clarified during initial meetings so that everyone is clear
on the plan of action. (Although questions are essential at
the onset of the project, the designer must continue to ask
questions throughout the design process, including inquiries
to the client and additional project participants, such as
proofreaders and printers.)

The primary goals and messages of the client (and the design)
need to be clearly defined in the project brief before moving
to the next stage of development—research and information
gathering. Restrictions, such as the budget, must also be
noted and assessed to determine their impact on the design.
Working with the client, the designer must establish the
project schedule, which includes imperative dates, such as
concept and design presentations, as well as deadlines and
delivery. It is important to share the project brief with all
participants to ensure that everyone understands the scope
of work and the plan for executing it.

In the development of the project brief, it is critical to consider
the role of the viewer. The client and designer must determine
to whom the project is directed. Understanding the target
audience shapes the direction of the design and dramatically
influences the end result. It is helpful to define the general
characteristics of the viewer, including age, geographic location, and general likes and dislikes. The designer must also
consider how the viewer will interact with the design so he
or she can choose a format that will allow the design to meet
the communication needs of the viewer. The viewer, although
not an active participant of the design process, will define
most of the designer's decision making.

establishing responsibilities While preparing the
project brief, the designer must begin to document and
gather the textual and visual elements used in the layout.
A clear assessment of all the elements will determine what
exists and what is needed to move forward with design
development. What the client and designer will each contribute to the content of the design also needs to be established and noted. If anything is missing, the designer must
ask the client to provide it. A running list of tasks to be
completed in a timely manner, such as contracting an illustrator or photographer, must be added to the project brief.
It is important for the designer to see the visual elements
that will be incorporated into the design in the early stages
of the process—this essential part of the project must be
defined as soon as possible.

The project brief outlines and establishes the relationship
and level of involvement between the client and designer
by specifying each of their roles. It is important to learn
how to interact with the client to avoid future pitfalls. Everyone involved with the project will adopt a certain amount
of responsibility, and it is wise to establish what is required
early in the process to avoid confusion when something
is needed. When the project brief is comprehensively completed, the designer can comfortably move to the next
stage of the design process.

THE PROJECT BRIEF

ADDRESSES THE DESIGN IN DETAIL AND INCLUDES EVERY ASPECT OF THE PROBLEM, AS WELL AS THE ROLES OF THE **CLIENT**, **DESIGNER**, AND **VIEWER**.

project brief functions

States the primary goals and messages of the design.

Provides a meticulous overview of the project.

Determines project restrictions, as well as the schedule and budget.

Outlines the client-designer relationship.

Establishes the responsibilities of everyone involved with the project.

Is used as a reference tool throughout the process.

Defines the characteristics of the viewer.

the actions of the client

Initiates the design project.

Determines the primary design objective.

Seeks returns from the design.

Respects the expertise of the designer.

Articulates anticipated outcomes and reactions.

Suggests the desired attitude of the design.

Prepares budgetary information.

Establishes deadlines for delivery.

Actively participates throughout the process.

Approves the design.

Provides feedback.

A series of questions, which can be tailored to address individual projects, provides a starting point to begin the project brief.

part one # the design problem

What type of project is needed (annual report, brochure, poster)?
What is the function and purpose of the design?
What are the client's objectives/goals for the design?
What is the primary message the client wants to communicate?
What considerations must be made to meet the needs of the client and viewer?
Are there any limitations or restrictions?
What is the budget?
What is the schedule?

part two # the client-designer relationship

What are the responsibilities of the client?
What are the responsibilities of the designer?
What is the level of client involvement?
In what stages of the design process will the client be directly involved?
What are the important dates, such as presentations and delivery?
How often will the client and designer interact?
What is the best method of communication (email, meetings, phone)?
Who are the primary contacts?

essentials of the client-designer relationship

respect

open communication

shared vision

trust

creative interaction

collaboration

part three # the viewer

Toward whom is the project directed?
What are the characteristics of the viewer?
What makes the viewer unique?
How will the viewer interact with the design?
What are the needs of the end user?

research and information-gathering

Following the preparation of the project brief, research and information-gathering is the second stage of the design process. It begins with a thorough review of all materials provided by the client. The designer must read, evaluate, and understand all the information presented in its entirety before he or she can intelligently work with it. Analyzing the content will increase the designer's knowledge of the topic and affect how the piece is designed. In addition, as the designer is educated about the topic, ideas will spark and the visualization process will begin. The more information the designer accumulates and digests, the greater the chance for the success of the project.

The designer should not rely solely on materials provided by the client. Additional research and information-gathering is often needed to expand the designer's familiarity with the topic beyond the initial client presentation. Independent research also broadens understanding and influences what the designer can bring to the design. The designer must acquire as much information as possible and, like the project brief, share the findings with relevant participants. Without thorough research and information-gathering, the design may be incomplete and lack a solid foundation.

research and information-gathering tips

Gain an understanding of the topic.

Read, evaluate, and understand all provided materials.

Independently research additional information.

Review the client's current communication materials.

Investigate competitive markets.

the client Another important step of the research and information-gathering stage is to review the client's current communication materials and strategies. This process leads to an awareness of how the client approaches their public image, as well as how they have positioned themselves visually in the past. It is helpful to discuss what the client likes and dislikes about their current communication materials and how they envision their evolution. Ask the client for examples of any prior materials, as well as competitive pieces that they find compelling and successful. This does not mean the client should request that the designer tailor the design based on other examples; rather, it provides the designer with a more complete understanding of the client and their perspectives on design. Bringing the client into the research and information-gathering stage is also a valuable way to foster a positive client-designer relationship. The client will feel like they are a part of the solution, whereas the designer will be able to take this opportunity to educate the client about design.

the competition Investigating the visual communication materials of competitive markets is another key component of the research and information-gathering stage. Understanding the market is critical to designing a piece that appropriately and effectively functions within it. Research can often prevent inadvertently designing a piece similar to a project already in existence. The designer must determine how the design will fit into the market and advance the needs of the client while simultaneously appealing to the viewer. Depending on the complexity of the project, professional researchers can be brought into the research and information-gathering stage to broaden the understanding of the business environment, as well as the specific requirements of the viewer.

Regardless of the scope of the project, research and information-gathering will enrich the designer and help achieve strong visual solutions. It must occur before brainstorming, conceptualization, or experimentation and development can begin. Research and information-gathering provides the knowledge base that will propel the design in the right direction.

brainstorming

Brainstorming is an expressive, problem-solving activity that promotes idea generation, helps the designer think about and work through complicated design problems, and encourages creative expression. Every thought and idea is valuable and worth recording. There are no right or wrong answers, no limitations to the process. Be inventive. Brainstorming ignites the mind of the designer who must think freely and openly—without restraint—to gain useful results.

Brainstorming can be performed individually or with a team of designers. Working collaboratively provides multiple points of view to the design problem, which can be more beneficial than a singular approach. Whereas one designer can brainstorm prolifically and conceive amazing solutions, a single perspective may sometimes be limiting. Engaging several thinkers in the process is a great way to obtain a broad perspective and initiate the development of thoroughly considered, innovative solutions. Occasionally, it is also helpful to invite the client into brainstorming sessions. This process educates the client and actively involves them in the design process while providing the designer with a practical point of view.

| *design* apt5a design group (Richard Bloom) |

Running lists of ideas and thoughts mark the brainstorming process for the Chronophonic CD. Inspired by the title, Footwork, *the list reflects the kinetic images used in the final design to connote the energy of the music.*

Inspiration boards are gathered collections of imagery that inspire and motivate the designer into action. They are useful tools that influence the direction of the design.

breakdancers

The Charleston

Flappers

'40s dancing

soccer players (jumping, kicking)

athletes jumping

jump shot

passing a player

long jump

dribbling up the court

hurdling

martial arts

wall-eye angle

jump kick

punching

flailing

celebrating

perspective of foot kicking close to camera

arms up

other dynamic perspectives

The brainstorming process may include producing freewritings, mind maps, and lists of ideas or thoughts, as well as creating visual inspiration boards. (Words and pictures equally contribute to brainstorming.) Stream-of-consciousness writing, or free-writing, helps the designer get thoughts immediately onto paper, whereas running lists record keywords and emotions associated with the design. Mind maps begin with one main idea placed in the center of a page with branches of subthemes extending out from the central theme. Each branch, or string of word associations, represents a new thought sequence. Inspiration boards combine selections of imagery that inspire and influence the direction of the design. After these initial brainstorming exercises, the broad scope of ideas must be reviewed, filtered, and developed into specific, workable ideas so the designer can move into the conceptualization stage.

brainstorming techniques

Practice freewriting.

Create mind maps.

Write down lists of thoughts and ideas.

Build visual inspiration boards.

| *design* 344 design, llc | *A collection of notes, brief writings, and sketches detail the idea-generation process that led to the design of the Solar Twins CD. Extensive preliminary thoughts and studies are imperative to the success of all designs; they ignite creativity and encourage intelligent, unique solutions.*

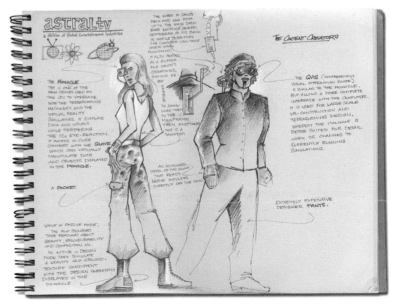

Mind mapping begins by placing a topic or theme in the center of a page and creating branches of thoughts that stem from the central keyword. It is a helpful method of visualizing the thought process while encouraging design development beyond initial ideas.

conceptualization

During the conceptualization stage of the design process, the designer must formulate the visual scheme, or plan, of the project. The concept is the thematic link between the design, its function, and the delivery of the message to the viewer; it is imperative to the success of the design. A strong concept will add depth to the project, while creating and maintaining viewer interest, providing focus, and promoting a cohesive visual solution. The designer must always consider the function of the design as well as its end user and must not overcomplicate the design with a concept that is inappropriate, unapproachable, or too abstract to deliver the message to the viewer. The design must be accessible, interesting, informative, and communicative.

three young boys to raise

and support

divorced after
ten years of marriage

Children's Home & Aid Society of Illinois 2003 Annual Report

this is helen

Helen had her job cut out for her. It was going to be pretty tough. She had no family close by to watch her boys. She had never left them with anyone else before, and didn't feel comfortable leaving them at any of the child care centers she had already visited. Coping with the aftermath of a divorce, finding someone to care for her boys who were 1, 2, and 9 years old, and finding a job so she could make ends meet created an overwhelming and frightening situation.

It became less so when she was able to enroll her two younger boys at Children's Home & Aid Society's child care center in Palatine. The staff was very helpful and gave her hope that things would work out. She found a job as a hostess in a restaurant and goes to work without worrying about her children. She feels that the children are receiving good meals at the center, and that they are loved and well cared for.

For Helen, the subsidized child care has helped her financial situation. But she feels that the staff at the center have been the biggest help of all. She feels that the children could not be at a better place. The staff noticed a speech delay in her youngest child, and arranged for the child to receive therapy at the center while Helen was at work. The convenient arrangement was an enormous help to Helen. Although it's a 50 minute drive to the center from her home, Helen feels the service is worth it.

Children's Home & Aid Society provides early childhood education and child care in Schaumburg, Palatine, Carpentersville, Bloomington, and Head Start and Early Head Start programs in Humboldt Park and Englewood.

| *design* samatamason | *Design concepts can be straightforward and objective. This annual report for the Children's Home & Aid Society of Illinois relies on the strength of the content to deliver the message; symbolism is not needed. Three true, personal stories are shared through the use of simple typography and candid photography. The sole purpose of the concept was to present the stories as clearly and efficiently as possible.*

The design can employ a number of approaches when shaping the concept of the design. If the content is clear and direct, the concept may result in an objective, straightforward visual solution. However, if the content is complicated with multiple types of information, the designer may develop a deeper conceptual direction that will better clarify the information. For example, the use of analogies and metaphors is an effective way to relay messages. Designers often use symbolism to help the viewer understand what the client is trying to communicate.

Regardless of the type of project, a singular, focused idea that drives the design must be determined at the end of the conceptualization stage. A solid design scheme will allow the designer to visualize the outcome of the piece, shift into the experimentation and development stage, and begin composing the visual elements with clarity.

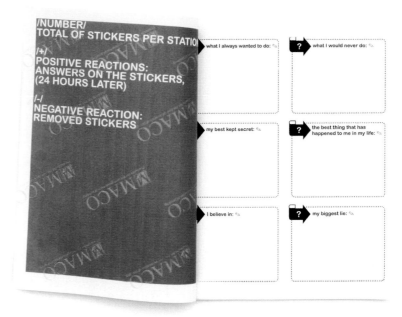

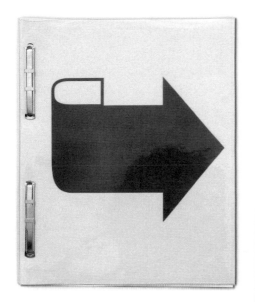

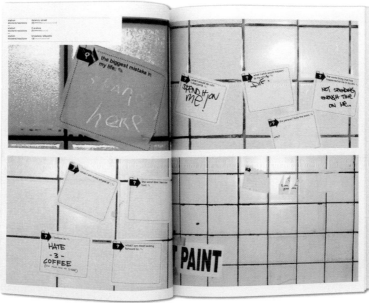

| *design* superbüro | *Progressive projects often rely on strong concepts. This book design is based on collecting and archiving the results of an experiment in which 300 stickers were placed in New York City subway tunnels asking people to react to questions. The format of the design is dictated by the idea of experiments. The metal binding connotes a notebook or chart in which to record results. Sheets of stickers are bound and displayed on their actual stock, whereas the final results are shown as snapshots that display the evidence. The message is delivered in a clinical, yet appropriate, fashion.*

experimentation and development

After the conceptualization stage, it is time to transform the visual elements into cohesive solutions. The experimentation and development stage follows a path from basic visual studies to refined variations. This stage begins with experimentation, which is important because it opens the mind of the designer and pushes his or her visual skills. Experimentation is a free, expressive process that is insightful and playful. Like brainstorming, the designer must not be restricted during the experimentation stage, because in most cases, the client will never see any of these initial studies. It is important to remember that experimentation does not need to generate definitive results. It may simply confirm that a new or more refined visual direction is the best solution.

During the experimentation stage, the designer can do a range of studies that include color, composition, and typography. For example, explore typefaces or develop a range of interchangeable color palettes. Consider diverse ways of handling illustration or photography. Examine the textual and visual content, and determine multiple ways of sequencing information. Test different grids and systems of proportion that structure the page. Introduce graphic shapes and linear elements. Additional options may include stepping away from the computer, working by hand, and passing the visual studies onto another designer for a fresh perspective and additional experimentation. Try anything different or new. Take the opportunity to be innovative. It can be comfortable, easy, and time efficient for the designer to revert to previously used solutions for design problems (especially under the stress of looming deadlines), but doing so will only create an inferior design. Experimentation is critical; it enhances the design process and encourages original solutions.

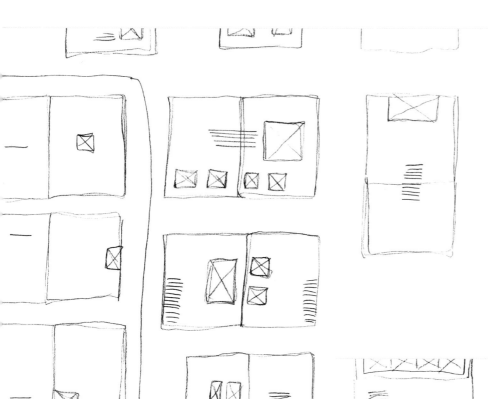

Thumbnail sketches are small, loose studies that quickly address basic compositional variations. Considering all the visual elements of the design, rough lines mark textual content and boxes indicate graphic shapes and imagery.

36

Through experimentation, the designer can test the strength of the concept as well as the visual investigations that work (or do not work). The designer should evaluate the preliminary studies based on comparative factors. By producing and assessing a range of visual work, the designer will be able to confidently select directions that have the greatest potential and then develop them into refined solutions. The value of experimentation is that it challenges the designer to think beyond the initial concept.

After evaluating the experimental studies, the designer must select the strongest directions for development. Thumbnail sketches that address the entire compositional space of the page, as well as the use of all visual elements, will help the designer quickly produce several variations. The thumbnails should be loose and created with rough lines marking typographic content, including paragraph settings, and boxes designating graphic shapes and imagery. Thumbnails can also indicate alignment points and relationships between elements on the page. Thumbnail sketching is a time-saving exercise and should be done before sitting down at the computer. Nothing is more productive than quick thumbnails that can be compared, eliminated, and developed.

During the experimentation stage, the thought process was open and free, and the visual studies were general and not reflective of the entire composition. However, in the development stage, multiple design solutions will come together and incorporate all the visual elements. The designer must now determine the primary grid or system of proportion that will structure and organize the design. Final typefaces must also be selected and implemented into a consistent, decisive typographic system to be applied throughout the design. The hierarchy of the design should be coordinated to logically lead the eye through dominant and subordinate levels of information. Compositionally, the space of the page must be controlled and exhibit dynamic, harmonious, and orchestrated solutions.

Producing variations of every design is essential during the development stage. Variations can be vastly different or merely subtle, with just slight changes in the proportions of the primary grid, typefaces and settings, diversified color palettes, or compositional factors, such as orientation and position. Each variation will allow the designer to compare the different directions and evaluate those that are strong or weak. In addition, the client often will want to see several variations before deciding on the final direction. Variations are the last component of the experimentation and development stage. At this point, the client and designer will select the option that is most suitable for refinement and completion during the execution stage.

experimentation ideas

Do multiple studies exploring color, composition, and typography.

Step away from the computer.

Develop several treatments for illustration or photography.

Sequence the textual and visual content in numerous ways.

Try anything different or new.

Introduce graphic shapes and linear elements.

Work by hand.

Pass the studies to another designer.

| *design* vrontikis design office |

Select experimental computer studies provide insight into the development of this poster. The studies are rough at this stage but successfully provide a range of options that includes both typographic and photographic solutions, as well as an interesting use of graphic shapes. Because an infinite number of solutions are available for all design problems, diverse exploration is essential.

PETRULA_A

IRONPIANIST
SPAININRIOT
PAINTSINRIO
NOASPIRINIT
RAISINPOINT
IANTIPRISON
ISOWRAINTIP
IPRINTISONA
INSPIRATION

PETRULA_B

IRONPIANIST
OTISPAIRINN
SPAININRIOT
PAINTSINRIO
NOASPRINIT
RAISINPOINT
INTRIOINSPA
ISOWRAINTIP
TONIINPARIS
IANTIPRISON
INAPRINTSO
INSPIRATION

PETRULA_C

IRONPIANIST
OTISPAIRINN
SPAININRIOT
PAINTSINRIO
NOASPRINIT
RAISINPOINT
INTRIOINSPA
ISOWRAINTIP
TONIINPARIS
IANTIPRISON
INAPRINTSO
INSPIRATION

PETRULA_D

IRONPIANIST
SPAININRIOT
PAINTSINRIO
NOASPIRINIT
RAISINPOINT
IANTIPRISON
ISOWRAINTIP
IPRINTISONA
INSPIRATION

PETRULA_E

IRONPIANIST
SPAININRIOT
PAINTSINRIO
IANTIPRISON
RAISINPOINT
NOASPIRINIT
ISOWRAINTIP
IPRINTISONA
INSPIRATION

| design vrontikis design office |

The next step of the development stage is creating variations based on the most effective solution chosen from the experimental studies. Variations can be vastly different (or subtle) with changes to the compositional factors, including color, orientation, position, and typography. In this example, the variations demonstrate the infinite range of options available when working in one focused direction. Comparing variations is an essential step in choosing the strongest solution.

execution

At this point in the design process, the concept has been finalized, and experimentation has resulted in a diverse set of exploratory studies. Additional development of the studies brought all the visual elements together into several variations, which were narrowed down to select the final direction. During the execution stage, the designer must examine every detail of the piece with a keen eye. He or she must preview the compositional space and organize the content logically and with sequential flow. Alignment, orientation, and position of the visual elements must be methodically coordinated to create appropriate relationships. The hierarchical system must ensure an ordered arrangement of textual and visual content with information designated into distinct levels of importance.

After working on a project, the designer is often attached to the piece, which sometimes makes it difficult for him or her to analyze the design objectively. As a result, it is helpful to present the design to others for evaluation of its visual presentation and utility. Is the design aesthetically strong? Does it demonstrate a consistent, unified system that applies to all the visual elements? Is the message of the piece clearly communicated? Will the viewer be able to use it effectively?

Review the project brief and use it as a checklist to determine if the final design successfully reflects the goals and function originally outlined. Be objective during this stage, and peruse the design carefully. In addition, ask the client to review the final design to ensure their satisfaction and approval of the visual solution before sending it to production. It is not too late to make changes that may improve the piece. In most cases, subtle refinements are often critical.

| **design** vrontikis design office |

At the end of the execution stage, the final design is reviewed carefully and objectively to ensure that all details are refined. In this example, subtle variations in color are assessed.

IRONPIANIST
SPAININRIOT
PAINTSINRIO
NOASPIRINIT
RAISINPOINT
IANTIPRISON
ISOWRAINTIP
IPRINTISONA
INSPIRATION

IT DOESN'T MATTER HOW YOU SPELL IT, OR DOES IT? INSPIRATION CAN COME
FROM ANYWHERE AND CAN MEAN INFINITE THINGS TO DIFFERENT PEOPLE.
JOIN DESIGNER, EDUCATOR, AND AUTHOR PETRULA VRONTIKIS WWW.35K.COM
TO EXPLORE PASSION, INSPIRATION, FOCUS, AND A PHILOSOPHY OF LEARNING.

FINAL THOUGHTS It is important to value and become engaged with each stage of the design process. A comprehensive methodology will provide a logical progression from the beginning to the end of a project. The designer will grow, learn, and improve with each design, whereas the design process, which is unique to every design (and designer), will become more acute through each new experience. Always remember to trust the process.

| *design* vrontikis design office |
The final design is the natural evolution of a thoroughly developed design process. Every stage is critical to ensuring appropriate and effective visual solutions.

for in-depth analysis information, refer to *chapter 8: design analysis* seeing the whole and its parts

There is a vitality, a life force,

a quickening that is translated through you into action,

and because there is only one of you in all time,

this expression is unique.

And if you block it,

it will never exist through any other medium,

and will be lost.

MARTHA GRAHAM
choreographer, dancer

INTUITION

Designers are creative thinkers and visual problem solvers.
Every project demands a different aesthetic and intellectual
approach to communicate appropriately, effectively, and
distinctively. Although basic design rules and techniques
must be learned, applied, and practiced, visual solutions
are not formulaic. Each designer contributes individual
knowledge, skills, experiences, and intuitive abilities to the
design process, which shape and distinguish all projects.
Unique to every designer, intuition enhances acuity and
dramatically influences the outcome of the final design.

design fundamentals and intuition

intuition defined

The fundamentals of design are universal. Color, form, and space, as well as structure, hierarchy, and typography, can be taught and learned. They are the foundation of design practice; their informed use must be inherent to the strength (and success) of the designer. There is no question that design education, whether formal or informal, is essential. However, understanding the fundamentals is only as effective as their application. Comprehension alone does not guarantee good design.

The basics of visual communication include visual language systems, structure and organization of compositional space, and hierarchy, as well as designing with color and typography. However, these basics do not specify methods for composing visual elements in all situations (there are far too many variables with each project). Certainly, there are a number of factors such as symmetry, figure-ground, position, and spatial relationships that influence compositional decision making. There is also a rich history of strong design examples to review and analyze. Yet, interestingly, no two designers will produce the same design, even when using identical content. In addition to experience and practice, intuition is the defining force that individualizes and separates one designer from the next. An innate sense for working with design fundamentals and composing the page is a critical component of the design process—it is the final piece of the puzzle.

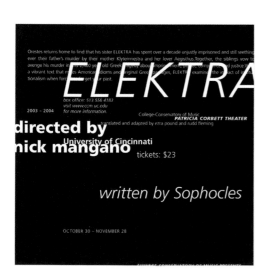

| design **heather sams** |

| design **paige strohmaier** |

| design **katherine varrati** |

Intuition is a different level of thinking, or cognition, that complements rational thought. It comes naturally and without hesitation, an immediate, involuntary insight that arrives unexpectedly without the influence or interference of rational thought. The inner voice, and the knowledge that it brings, is independent and unexplainable, yet is always present. In a general sense, intuition leads and protects, enlightens and inspires. It synthesizes brain impulses, whether innate or learned, and brings forth new and unexpected thoughts that would not emerge through logical reasoning.

connecting the conscious and subconscious

Intuition is the unpredictable connection that bridges the gap between the conscious and subconscious mind; the subconscious provokes the arrival of wisdom into consciousness. Intuition strikes at any time (even if it arrives unnoticed), and is informed by past experiences, both remembered and forgotten, which are stored in memory. It is also influenced by the present and anticipation of future events. It stems from dreams, imagination, and inspiration, and can be sparked by the everyday environment, which constantly influences and stimulates the brain. Although it is not fully understood and is difficult to verbalize, intuition works for the benefit of the designer with meaning and purpose.

the influence of rational thinking

Rational thinking analyzes and questions all thoughts. Though essential to the design process, logical reasoning can sometimes inadvertently suppress intuition and prevent the designer from exploring new creative opportunities. For example, the need to justify every action (and the fear attached with not being able to do so) often discourages the designer from responding to and trusting his or her gut. The designer believes that reacting to intuition invalidates the design and makes it careless, flighty, or too abstract. The inexperienced designer doubts instincts and strictly relies on learned knowledge that he or she believes is absolute; or, the designer finds it difficult to trust the effectiveness of the design unless the intellect behind it is thoroughly explained. The designer is concerned that a methodology that includes intuition is unrelated to the practical needs of the client and viewer. These concerns are reasonable, yet none negate the positive influence of intuition. Intuition works in conjunction with learned knowledge and rational thinking to achieve effective solutions. The addition of intuition takes the design a step further.

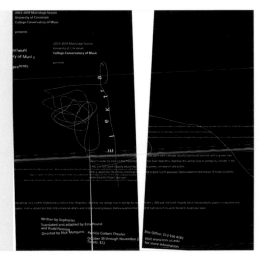

| design hans schellhas |

This collection of typographic studies demonstrates the unlimited range of solutions to one design problem. Each designer was given the same specifications, including page format, grid, text, and typeface. Through the exploration of hierarchy, compositional factors, and objective and subjective representation, as well as the individual influence of intuition, the designers developed unique and varied solutions.

intuitive functions

guidance

protection

inspiration

enlightenment

synthesis

the benefits of intuition

Designers are naturally inclined to creativity. Intuition is beneficial because it cultivates imagination and allows the designer to move beyond his or her comfort zone, thereby increasing the potential of the designer (and the design). It can lead to fresh and innovative solutions or strengthen the aesthetic, concept, and visual presentation of the design. Intuition increases the number of ideas that are generated and provides the spark to push the design beyond expectations. In addition, intuition eases decision making for the designer and influences the composition of the visual elements. The inner voice, or gut reaction, informs the designer about what works in the development of compelling, effective, and communicative layouts. However, the designer must also know that intuition alone does not dictate effective solutions—it is a supporting factor and helps the designer through a logical process.

THE **INNER VOICE**, OR GUT REACTION,

| *design* hendersonbromsteadartco. |

Intuition enhances creative potential and leads to fresh, innovative solutions that exceed expectation. In the poster for Triad Health Project, an AIDS service-and-support organization, intuition helped define the "campy and tongue-in-cheek" attitude. Art director Hayes Henderson adds, "You see a problem and you say, 'This is what you need to do!' It's just built in. Everybody's got one."

nurturing intuition Intuition requires nurturing to become a productive component of the design process. The designer must respond to his or her immediate feelings and bursts of insight without worrying about the final outcome. It takes time and practice to believe that instincts are valuable. Whereas rational thinking is powerful and reliable, intuitiveness is equally commanding. (Relying solely on rational thinking sometimes results in repetitive solutions and stale, boring design.) Trusting intuition encourages the designer to take chances—risk taking adds vitality to the design and a certain sense of the unexpected. The designer must react to intuitive sense and test it out through experimentation to see how it fits into and relates to the design problem (if at all).

Intuitiveness is cultivated in numerous ways. The designer must be careful not to analyze the suggestions of the inner voice before testing them out. It is useful to go through the process of experimentation, even if the insights seem impractical. Do not abandon or prejudge their worth. (Reason will counter many gut reactions and stifle intuition.) The designer must also continue fostering intuition through active involvement during the design process, as well as in activities and environments outside of design. Take periodic breaks to take the mind off the project. Try collecting thoughts verbally and visually. Actively seek out inspiration, which stimulates idea generation. Expect the unexpected and be open to anything. Ask questions and be informed. Always feed the subconscious to enhance its effectiveness. With experience, the designer learns to decipher the helpful insights from insignificant ones.

INFORMS THE DESIGNER ABOUT WHAT WORKS IN THE DEVELOPMENT OF **COMPELLING**, **EFFECTIVE**, AND **COMMUNICATIVE** LAYOUTS.

breaking the myths of intuition

Learned knowledge is enhanced by intuition.

Intuition should not be feared, doubted, or mistrusted.

Intuition does inform the design process.

Intuition does not invalidate the design.

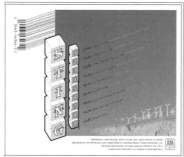

| **design** 344 design, llc | *This set of fifteen variations, as well as the final solution (facing page), for the* Sting Brand New Day: The Remixes *CD demonstrates how intuition ignites creativity and increases the number of ideas generated for design problems. "Intuition is my design process,"* notes designer Stefan Bucher. *Experimentation and exploration are key factors that stimulate the subconscious and prompt the arrival of useful instincts.*

nurturing intuition

Actively listen and react to the inner voice.

Do not be afraid to take risks.

Learn to trust feelings and insights.

Test intuitive thoughts to understand their value.

Expect the unexpected.

Do not overanalyze intuition.

Do not abandon or prejudge instinctive ideas.

Experiment.

Take periodic breaks when working on a project.

Be open-minded.

Ask questions and be informed.

Record thoughts and collect visuals.

Seek out inspiration.

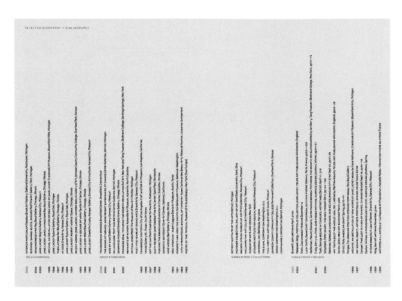

SELECTED BIOGRAPHY + BIBLIOGRAPHY

understanding the limits Although its advantages are great, intuition is not always useful or appropriate. The reliance on intuition does not negate a thorough design methodology from inception to completion of the project. Some insights are completely impractical and useless, with no effect on design development. Remember that intuitiveness contributes to the design, but it does not determine its success or failure. The designer still needs to be fully aware of and meet the project objectives. He or she cannot refute constructive criticism because the design claims to be inspired by intuition. If the pragmatic focus is lost because of the influence of intuition, the design is purposeless and insights ineffective.

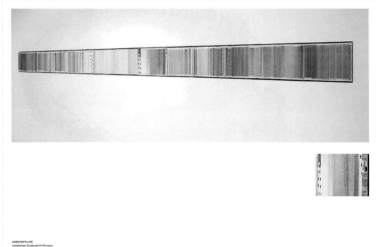

| *design* concrete [the office of jilly simons] | *Contemplating the design of* Interior Particular [Jane Lackey], *an exhibition catalogue featuring Lackey's work, designer Jilly Simons explains, "Intuition usually plays a large role in many of my solutions. You may research and study, but ultimately, the faculty of sensing beyond the use of rational processes often provides that which may not be evident."*

WEBSTER'S LINE
installation, Cranbrook Art Museum
1999
9.5 x 160 x 1.75 inches
dictionary pages, polyurethane

| design 33rpm | *Discussing the Yeah Yeah Yeahs poster, designer Andrio Abero states, "I thought about the concept more than I usually do with other posters, but my choices of imagery were intuitive, especially the hand and tweezers. Intuition is what makes my designs stand out. If it looks right and I feel it's strong enough, that's when I output the film for it to be printed. Intuition means being experimental. How else will your skills as a designer grow?"*

FINAL THOUGHTS Intuition is the creative force that leads the designer by helping him or her make choices that affect the design process from conceptualization to execution. In combination with learned knowledge, intuitiveness encourages solutions that can range from the ordinary to the unconventional. Incorporating intuition into the process allows the designer to tap into and investigate unknown depths of his or her abilities. Its value grows as the designer accepts, trusts, and follows his or her instincts time and again.

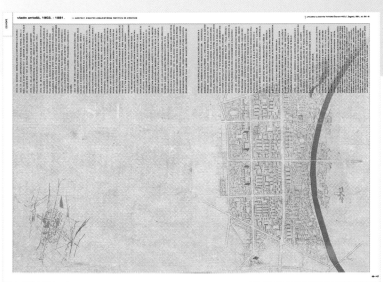

| design cavarpayar | *"In the design process, there are things that you think about rationally, those you learn about, and those you are looking for," says designer Lana Cavar on spreads from CIP magazine. "And then, there is the most interesting part [of the process] you cannot be rational about. You just feel it for some strange reason. If you feel right, it will fit into the concept perfectly and make it more interesting and unique."*

STRUCTURE

...human activity itself has

since the earliest times, **been distinguished by the quest for order.**

JOSEF MÜLLER–BROCKMAN
author, graphic designer, teacher, typographer

ORGANIZATION

BUILDING FOUNDATIONS

The word *grid* is used to define the structural force behind the design. Grids are organizational tools that define the active space of the page and help the designer make thoughtful decisions about composition and order. Grids enable the designer to maintain control, create visual connections, and unify the design.

grid systems in graphic design

Simply stated, grids are a series of intersecting axes that create horizontal and vertical divisions of space on the page. These intervals accommodate the placement of the visual elements, which, if positioned effectively, create movement across, down, within, and outside the surface of the page. The designer arranges the visual elements to interact, rather than conflict, establishing a pathway through the design that reveals dominant and subordinate levels of information. The designer is in complete control—visual elements are composed on gridded surfaces with assigned voices that, in combination with others (from whispers to shouts), are visually melodic.

| **design** kristin cullen | The grid is an active element of this letterhead system, which contrasts control and order with expression and intuition. Imagery emerges from visual grid lines to reflect process. Minimal and sophisticated typography is aligned along the columns and margins, making the grid intentionally implied without being seen.

| **design** sumo | The cover of the Northern Film & Media Location Guide combines beautiful imagery with an elegant type treatment that subtly mimics the image it overlays. The physical shape of the booklet connotes environments, landscapes, and vistas, which is conceptually appropriate to the content that lies inside.

Grids vary in size and shape from simple to complex, depending on the range and amount of information that must be incorporated into the design. Always developed with the content in mind, grids are reinvented with every project. They are modeled after structures and systems of proportion found in architecture, fine art, mathematics, music, and nature; grids are also informed by the instinct of the designer. Theorized throughout history by the likes of Pythagoras, Vitruvius, Michelangelo, Leonardo da Vinci, and Le Corbusier, common systems of proportion include the Fibonacci sequence, the golden section, and modular scales. Whether mathematical or intuitive, grids are devoted to cohesion and harmony.

Falsely seen as restrictive, grids allow diverse visual elements to coexist. Visual elements are mutually dependent on their relationship to each other to communicate comprehensive messages. Flexibility is inherent in grids, providing unlimited creative opportunities for the designer. Remember, grids do not dictate the design or its outcome. They work with, rather than against, the intentions of the designer. The designer uses, adapts, breaks, and abandons grids for the benefit of the design. The skilled and experienced designer composes the visual elements gracefully or clumsily and determines if the design is active or static, compelling or boring, communicative or uninformative.

01	INTRODUCTION	02	COUNTRYSIDE
02	WHO HAS CHOSEN THE NORTH EAST	08	COAST, HARBOURS AND RIVERS
		13	CASTLES
		18	HERITAGE
		24	LANDMARKS
		26	BRIDGES
		29	ON THE MOVE
		31	NORTHERN LIVING
		36	CITIES
		40	INDUSTRY

THE NORTH-EAST IS THE MOST WONDERFUL PLACE IN THE ENTIRE WORLD. IT'S ALSO HOME TO THE NICEST PEOPLE.

This is a self-evident truth, especially if, like me, you come from there.

As for the rest of humanity, for years it's been said that the region is Britain's best-kept secret but lately, thanks to diverse and highly successful movies like Robin Hood, Prince of Thieves, Elizabeth, Billy Elliot and Harry Potter, the word is out.

Tourists are flocking to the region for the same reason that film-makers do – there is a staggering range of landscapes and man-made features – everything from Roman ruins to wonderful beaches, epic moorland to medieval castles and cathedrals. From the point of view of the producer or location-hunter, there is very little that can't be found in the North-East, including crews with the right skills, amenable local authorities and friendly folk to act as extras.

I could throw some statistics at you, like the fact that my vibrant home city (Newcastle) has more hotel rooms per capita than any other city in the UK, but my central message is – come! You will be made very welcome. In the meantime, we at Northern Film & Media have tried to make this book comprehensive. We hope you find it useful.

Michael Chaplin, Chair
June 2003

Elizabeth Karsen, Mumbo Jumbo (Purely Better)

| **design** sumo | *An interior spread demonstrates the flexibility of multiple-column grids. Imagery changes in scale and position along the vertical alignment points to provide contrast, rhythm, and variation throughout the design.*

| **design** sumo | *The structure of the design is introduced on the first spread. Dividing the page into multiple columns enables a systematic arrangement of the visual elements. Although the horizontal flow of the spread is flexible to accommodate text and imagery of variable widths, the starting point of all elements consistently begins from the top margin.*

the anatomy of grids

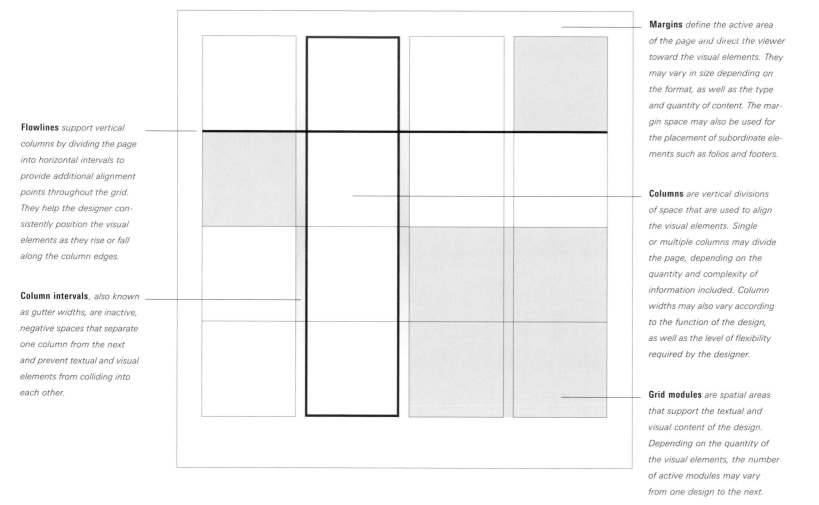

Flowlines *support vertical columns by dividing the page into horizontal intervals to provide additional alignment points throughout the grid. They help the designer consistently position the visual elements as they rise or fall along the column edges.*

Column intervals*, also known as gutter widths, are inactive, negative spaces that separate one column from the next and prevent textual and visual elements from colliding into each other.*

Margins *define the active area of the page and direct the viewer toward the visual elements. They may vary in size depending on the format, as well as the type and quantity of content. The margin space may also be used for the placement of subordinate elements such as folios and footers.*

Columns *are vertical divisions of space that are used to align the visual elements. Single or multiple columns may divide the page, depending on the quantity and complexity of information included. Column widths may also vary according to the function of the design, as well as the level of flexibility required by the designer.*

Grid modules *are spatial areas that support the textual and visual content of the design. Depending on the quantity of the visual elements, the number of active modules may vary from one design to the next.*

Smaller margins increase the active area of the composition. They are useful when working with multiple-column or modular grids, which accommodate complex designs with a variety of visual elements.

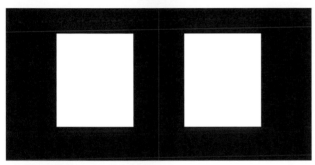

Larger margins decrease the active space of the page but increase the amount of white space. Ample margins provide a stable composition and direct the viewer toward the positive areas of the design, while also leaving finger room to hold the piece.

| ***design* lichtwitz** | *In this catalogue design, margins are broken to allow typography to move off the page. The implied movement expands the visual environment outside the surface of the page and provides sequential flow from one page to the next.*

margins Margins define the active area of the compositional space and direct the viewer toward the visual elements. Margins can vary in size depending on the format of the page, as well as the textual and visual content of the design. Left and right, as well as top and bottom, margins can be equal all around or larger and smaller, depending on the proportions of the page. On double-page spreads, the inside margins must be large enough so that nothing is lost in the gutter. In addition, the margin space can be used for the placement of subordinate elements, including folios and footers.

Smaller margins increase the usable surface area of the composition, which accommodates complex designs with various visual elements. For example, in this book, small left- and right-side margins extend the active space of the page to support considerable amounts of textual and visual content on each spread. (Multiple columns divide the compositional space.) Larger margins decrease the active space of the page but increase the amount of white space, creating an open visual environment that is approachable, inviting, and soothing. For example, books of continuous text without extensive visuals benefit from large margins. Ample margins provide a stable compositional space that directs the viewer toward the positive areas of the design, while also leaving finger room to hold the piece.

Margins are not intended to trap the visual elements within the compositional space; they are used to activate the positive areas of the design. In many cases, the outer margins can be broken to allow the visual elements to move off the page. The implied movement expands the visual environment outside of the composition.

columns Columns are vertical divisions of space used to align the visual elements. Single or multiple columns can divide the page, depending on the quantity of textual and visual information. Columns can also be distributed evenly across the page. In other cases, column widths can vary according to the specific content and function of the design, as well as the amount of desired compositional flexibility. (It is a general rule that more columns, or spatial divisions, foster additional flexibility for the arrangement of the visual elements.)

column intervals Column intervals are the spatial divisions that reside between columns. They are much smaller in width than columns and prevent collisions of textual and visual information by providing an inactive negative space that separates one column from the next. Column intervals are critical when the visual elements juxtapose in the same position from column to column. For example, if continuous text is broken into side-by-side columns, the column interval prevents the viewer from moving from the line of one paragraph into the line of the paragraph next to it.

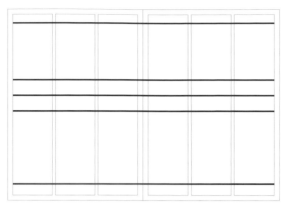

| *design* no.parking | A three-column grid accommodates a range of text, including words, lines, and paragraphs. The simple structure also includes three central flowlines, as well as one at the top and bottom, which provide alignment points for the composition of text, graphic shapes, and imagery. Column intervals also provide breathing room between juxtaposed columns of continuous text.

flowlines Flowlines divide the page into horizontal spatial divisions and create additional alignment points for the placement of the visual elements. They are guides that help the designer establish consistent alignment across and down the page. Flowlines dictate the horizontal positions of visual elements and how they rise or fall along the column edges.

grid modules Grid modules are active spatial fields that accommodate the placement of the visual elements. The designer can assign specific modules for textual content and imagery and apply this system throughout the design. Doing so creates consistency because the viewer can expect to see similar information positioned in the same grid modules. When assigning grid modules, be careful to avoid monotony. Although repeating the position of visual elements helps maintain consistency, it can also diminish the active, rhythmic sequence of the design. The designer can also choose to work more loosely and vary the position of the textual and visual content that appears in the grid modules intentionally. This increases the harmony, rhythm, and tension of the design and eliminates ineffective repetition and predictability.

| **design** gravica design/talisman interactive | *Modular grids can accommodate a range of visual elements. In this example, the grid, which is divided into nine square modules, is evident. The designer has chosen to crop imagery based on the module proportion, and the text spans the length of two units. The type size has been adjusted appropriately to fit the measure without sacrificing readability.*

working with basic grids

development and application A solid, well-planned foundation is an imperative starting point in the development of the design. A number of grid options are available to the designer, but they all serve the same primary function. Grids allow the designer to intelligently control and organize the compositional space and orchestrate the visual elements dynamically, rhythmically, and harmoniously in relationship to each other. Spatial connections are established that direct the eye toward positive space and effectively lead the viewer through the composition.

The goal of working with grids is to order and unify the compositional space; the underlying structure should be apparent without actually being seen. The designer must compose the visual elements to balance and contrast the shape of the page, while also providing the viewer with a clear sense of direction and movement through the design. The designer encourages viewer interaction and readability through dynamic visual compositions. It is important to experiment with grids with a playful sensibility, but use them wisely.

THE PERFECT WEEKEND
→ **FRIDAY** PULL INTO LILLE-EUROPE STATION IN TIME FOR DINNER, AND TAKE A TAXI TO LOW-KEY L'ORANGE BLEUE. DRINKS AT CHEZ MOREL, BEFORE BEDDING DOWN AT HOTEL BRUEGHEL OR L'HERMITAGE, DEPENDING ON YOUR BUDGET. → **SATURDAY** BREAKFAST AT PAUL ON THE GRAND' PLACE. SHOP IN COBBLED VIEUX LILLE WITH A LIGHT LUNCH AT ESTAMINET 'T RIJSEL. TOUR THE PALAIS DES BEAUX ARTS AND BUY POSTCARDS OF YOUR FAVOURITE PAINTINGS. SPLURGE ON DINNER AT A L'HUITRIÈRE - NO CONTEST. AFTERWARDS, QUIET DRINKS AT L'ILLUSTRATION, SAPO FOR A COCKTAIL SCENE, LA SCALA FOR DANCING. → **SUNDAY** BEELINE TO WAZEMMES MARKET TO FIND A BARGAIN. EAT AT PAIN ET VIN, BEFORE TAKING THE METRO TO ROUBAIX [MUSEUM OF ART AND INDUSTRY] OR VILLENEUVE D'ASCQ [MODERN ART MUSEUM]. LATE AFTERNOON TEA AT BELLE ÉPOQUE SALON MÉERT OR A QUICK DINNER AT LA PART DES ANGES. HURRY TO THE STATION 30MIN BEFORE DEPARTURE.

SHOPPING → SNIFF OUT THE CHEESE SHOP THAT SUPPLIES NUMBER 10, THE WHITE HOUSE AND MOST IMPORTANTLY, FRANCE'S ELYSÉE PALACE.

MARKETS → Lille has three markets: the first, Provençale-style **Marché Place du Concert** offers the stuff food dreams are made of. Like fresh foie gras costing about €17/kg. Have a coffee at Café aux Arts. Market days Wed/Fri/Sun 8am-2pm.

The second market is the cutest, in the courtyard of the 17th-century **Bourse** (stock exchange) selling books, stamps and cigarette cards. Market days Tues-Sun 11am-7pm approx. Take Metro Line 1 to Gambetta, and get lost in the vast fleamarket **Marché de Wazemmes**. Vendors peddle food, clothes, antiques and animals, flanked on all sides by little bistros and cafés. Stop by three favourites on Place de la Nouvelle Aventure. La Brûlerie for strong coffee...next door Tiparo Thai offers spring rolls and dumplings to passing trade, beside Pain et Vin, serving delicious tartines. Market days Tue/Thu/Sun 7am-2pm.

EURALILLE → Urban architect Rem Koolhaas created the shopping/entertainment complex between the old railway station and the new Lille-Europe station. It's a thoroughly modern mall, choc-a-with the familiar brand names.

VIEUX LILLE → One-off shopping is in cobbled **Old Lille**, around rue de la Monnaie (the town's oldest street). Stores like Anne Fontaine (white shirts), Aigle (outdoor wear), as well as Kenzo, Deschamps, Hermès and Louis Vuitton. Favourites include: **Philippe Olivier** Take home local

Maroilles or dried out Vieilles Mimolette from this world-famous fromagerie (3 rue du Curé St Etienne). **Sade** All things nice, like lovely silky dresses and sexy one-off tops (3 rue de la Monnaie). **Atelier Un Vrai Semblance** Guillaume Mosson has his own repertoire of canvases but also works on commission, creating copies of the masters, trompe l'oeil for your walls and portraits of your fair self (3 rue au Péterinck). **Tambours et Trompettes** The French know best how to dress kiddiwinks. Here, Valérie Ferrion can make the grubbiest of toddlers achingly pretty (14 rue au Péterinck).

| *design* wilsonharvey/loewy |

This pocket-size travel guide demonstrates the use of a four-column grid. Small margins increase the active area for the composition of the visual elements. Elements can fit comfortably into one column measure or run across the entire page.

Grid proportions and spatial relationships are determined by the page format, as well as the complexity of the visual elements. Grids should be tailored to accommodate specific visual elements. If grids are arbitrarily developed without consideration of the textual and visual content, the designer will encounter difficulties. Arbitrary grids can become too dictatorial or loose, force thoughtless decisions, or provide too few or many spatial divisions to accommodate all the necessary content. Without clear focus and development, grids will limit the designer, instead of providing the foundation to construct an effective, meaningful design.

the functions of grids

control

organization

rhythm

harmony

unity

dynamism

readability

movement

balance

direction

contrast

interaction

order

| **design** aufuldish & warinner |

Yellow fields of color are used to reinforce the structure and call attention to the text within, which is composed throughout the design in columns of varying width. The graphic shapes define the margins, as well as the columns and column intervals, which are easily detected. The flexible grid adds variety and rhythm from page to page.

single-column grids

single-column grids Single-column grids are the most basic structural systems. They provide a simple compositional framework suitable for presenting large amounts of continuous text. The space of the page is defined by the margins, which divides the active area into one column. For example, a classical approach is common. Classical margins are large on the sides and bottom and smaller at the top. The inner margin is typically half the size of the outer margin. In addition, the positions of the columns on the spread are mirrored. However, the column can also be repeated on the facing page in the same position to create an asymmetric composition.

Margins are the primary consideration of single-column grids and need adjustment to improve the appearance of the visual elements, especially the text. The single column should not be too wide or narrow and must accommodate an appropriate line length for effective readability. Typeface selection, size, and leading must be carefully considered to achieve optimal results.

A 2:3 classical page proportion for a single-column grid is appropriate for large amounts of continuous text. When working with one column, determining the ideal typeface, size, line length, and leading is imperative. Traditionally, the columns mirror each other to create a balanced, symmetrical presentation. An alternative is to repeat the column position on the facing page to create asymmetry and provide a contemporary feel.

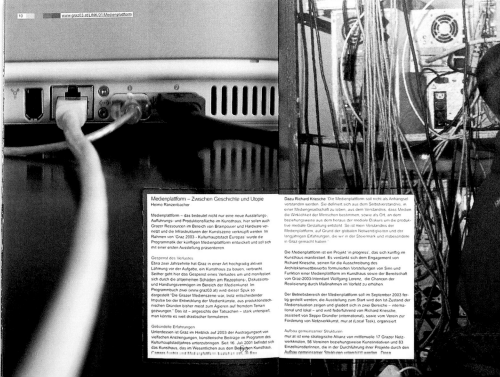

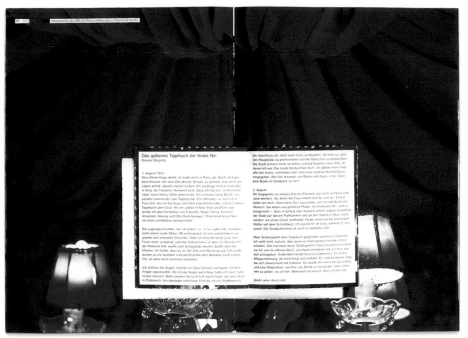

| **design lichtwitz** | *Generous margins
are filled with photography, which
provides a dynamic background for
single columns of text. The open
margins are spacious and direct the
eye to the text, which is pushed
toward the center and bottom of the
page. The margins create dramatic
tension that is used effectively
in the symmetrical composition.*

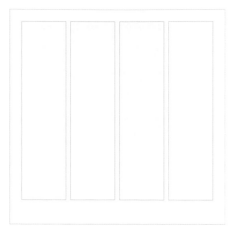

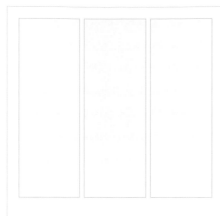

Multiple-column grids are divided into several intervals. Columns increase flexibility and provide unlimited compositional options. Complex projects, which require the interaction of diverse visual elements, are perfect candidates for multiple-column grids.

multiple-column grids Multiple-column grids contain several spatial intervals, which provide endless compositional options. They are flexible and accommodate a range of visual elements. Multiple-column grids are suitable for complex projects, including books, magazines, and publications that contain diverse content. The quantity of textual and visual content, as well as the page format, will help the designer determine the ideal number of intervals.

Multiple-column grids provide opportunities to create rhythm, drama, movement, and tension through the interaction of visual elements. For example, textual and visual elements can reside in several columns, span the page, overlap other elements, rest on fields of color or texture, or run off the page. (Scale, orientation, and position variations promote hierarchy and contrast in multiple-column grids.) However, be cautious—too many divisions of space and activity can lead to confusion and disorder.

| design renate gokl | In this newsletter, a multiple-column grid is used effectively and dynamically. The structure is evident and reinforced through linear elements and graphic shapes that align along column edges and connect the visual elements. The use of white space is also proficient, whereas changes in the scale of imagery, typography, and line length provides depth and rhythm.

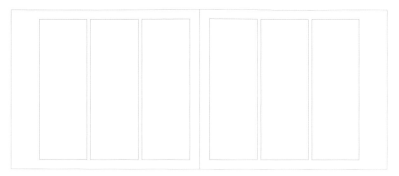

| **design** enspace | A three-column grid defines the structure of this annual report. The simple system is accessible and provides a clear presentation of information. Body text fits into the one-column measures, whereas larger headline text spans the width of two columns. Generous left and right margins provide ample finger room to hold the piece.

CONSTELLATIONS OF COLLABORATION.

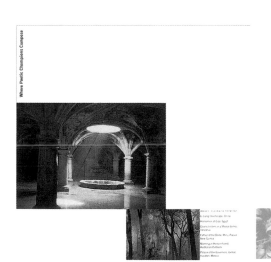

modular grids Modular grids are an extension of multiple-column grids with the addition of horizontal flowlines, which divide the page into spatial units or modules. Modules are the active areas of the page that accommodate the visual elements. Because the number and size of the spatial units is dictated by the content, the designer must assess the amount of text and imagery to determine the appropriate module shape. For example, the size of a module could be determined by the ideal width, or line length, of the body copy (it can span multiple modules), as well as the smallest possible size of a photograph or illustration.

Like multiple-column grids, modular grids increase compositional flexibility and are also suitable for publications, including magazines and newspapers. It is often the case that modular grids are components of extensive visual language systems, which means that the grid is applied to multiple pieces over time. The grid must be flexible enough to accommodate changing content while maintaining the ability to be understood and easily adapted by several designers.

Modular grids divide the page into horizontal and vertical spatial units called modules, which are the active areas of the composition that accommodate the visual elements. The designer gains increased flexibility as the number of modules grows. However, too many modules can be confusing and lead to chaos.

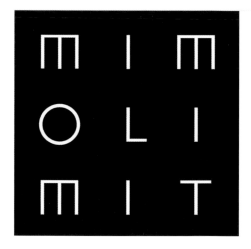

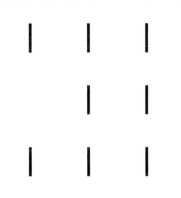

mimolimit

*| **design** studio najbrt | A minimal design is supported by a simple structure. The limited amount of content is suited to a nine-unit modular grid. Modular grids offer consistency for the placement of visual elements. For example, the dominant typographic content falls from the top of the second set of horizontal modules, whereas the subordinate text hangs from the third.*

bubble club   2001

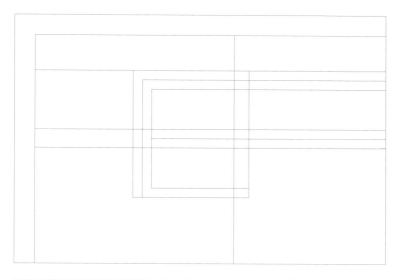

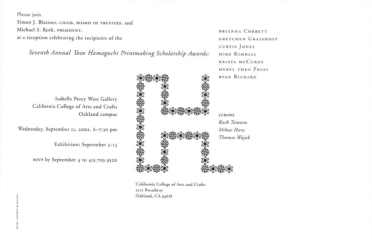

Please join
Simon J. Blattner, CHAIR, BOARD OF TRUSTEES, and
Michael S. Roth, PRESIDENT,
at a reception celebrating the recipients of the

Seventh Annual Yozo Hamaguchi Printmaking Scholarship Awards:

BRIANNA CORBETT
GRETCHEN GRASSHOFF
CURTIS JONES
MIKE KIMBALL
KRISTA McCURDY
MERYL THEO PRESS
RYAN RICKARD

Isabelle Percy West Gallery
California College of Arts and Crafts
Oakland campus

Wednesday, September 11, 2002, 6–7:30 pm

JURORS
Ruth Tamura
Mikae Hara
Thomas Wujak

Exhibition: September 3–13

RSVP by September 4 to 415.703.9520

California College of Arts and Crafts
5212 Broadway
Oakland, CA 94618

| ***design** aufuldish & warinner* |

*The H is a decisive focal point
and provides the structure
around which most of the textual content aligns. The basic
grid is reinvented. The edges
and lines of the dominant
shape create horizontal and
vertical divisions of space.*

alternative grids Alternative grids are often loose and organic and rely heavily on the intuitive placement of the visual elements. (Intuition plays an important role when working with all grids—it helps the designer make choices and keeps them attuned to what works and what does not.) They are often used when basic grids are not needed or if the content requires more spatial complexity. Alternative grids can evolve from any of the basic grids by taking them apart and adding, deleting, overlapping, or shifting the spatial divisions.

All visual elements are inherently structural. In alternative grids, the visual elements define the architecture of the page, as well as the spatial relationships between elements. For example, the compositional structure is built around the dominant visual element, or focal point, using its lines, orientation, and position as alignment points for additional elements. Alternative grids require attention to ensure that the visual elements are working together. The use of an alternative grid, or lack of a grid, does not negate the need for an ordering system. Spatial relationships and visual connections are imperative in all grids and help the viewer navigate through the design.

Swimming Lessons:

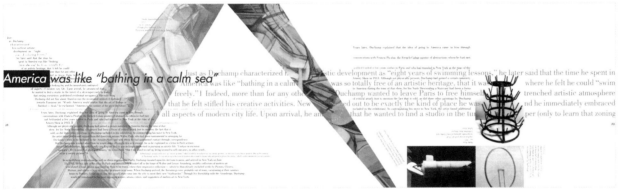

| *design* jennifer pfeiffer | *Two columns and flowlines of a basic horizontal and vertical grid are rotated approximately 30 degrees to invigorate the space of the page. Strong diagonal alignment points are established and become the dominant structural force of the design. Text, imagery, and graphic shapes are integrated and create activity and movement.*

America was like "bathing in a calm sea"

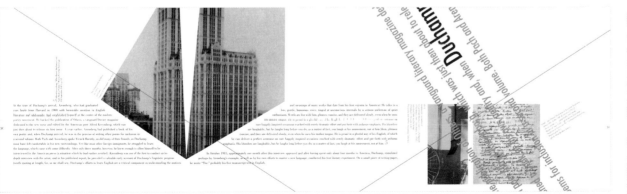

breaking the grid No grids (or rules) are absolute. There are numerous paths that lead to appropriate, dynamic, and effective visual solutions. Grids provide the basis, as well as innumerable options, to construct strong layouts. Experience, practice, and experimentation lead to productive results. Although grids provide the foundation to build the design, the designer must also learn that grids can be broken and abandoned with a controlled, intelligent hand. Relying too heavily on the grid sometimes leads to poor compositional choices. The designer must control the composition using the grid as a guide instead of the dictator of the layout. As such, the designer must break the grid in small or large increments for the benefit of the design. However, if the grid is broken too often, it may indicate that it is not suitably developed for the content.

| **design** patrick crawford | *In this typographic study, multiple diagonals interrupt a basic eight-column grid and dictate a new structure. The grid needed to be broken to provide better focus and navigation through the design, which represents a journey around a town square. Angular elements contrast with the horizontal elements and lead the viewer through the compositional space.*

Grids are tremendous assets to layout development, but they are not the definitive answer to successful design solutions. They must be used with acute skill, in conjunction with decisive hierarchy, typographic application, and interaction of visual elements. The designer should use grids freely, adhere to spatial divisions to create dynamic relationships, and intelligently break them when appropriate. If viewed as restrictive, the grid (and the designer) will never be used to its fullest potential.

| **design** resist imposters | Loose, organic compositions can be visually appealing and hierarchically strong without evidence of a grid. Without a grid, it is important to create connections among the visual elements. This poster logically begins at the top center of the page with the name Denali. The stem provides a strong axis that leads the eye toward the subordinate information.

| **design** kearneyrocholl | The traditional grid is challenged in this poster. Playing off the angular diamond form, typographic elements are composed within its triangular shapes. The challenge of this alternative grid is working within the triangular divisions of space and finding enough surface area to compose the text.

THE INTERACTION

The white surface of the paper is taken to be 'empty,'

an inactive surface,

despite visible structures that are present.

With the first appearance of a dot,

a line,

ADRIAN FRUTIGER
illustrator, teacher, type and graphic designer, typographer

the empty surface is activated.

OF **VISUAL ELEMENTS**

ESTABLISHING HIERARCHY

The blank page is dull, meaningless, and static, yet full of potential. To the designer, it is an empty canvas used to create meaning. Color, form, image, space, and typography collaborate to convey an intended message. When the designer activates the page through the placement of the visual elements, he or she needs an ordering system to help the viewer make sense of the design. The ordering system, or hierarchy, defines the level of activity and importance for every visual element and determines their sequence through the design. Dominant and subordinate visual elements are composed decisively to achieve clarity. No visual element is insignificant; each one contributes in overt and subtle ways to the communication of the message. A strong, systematic hierarchy provides accessibility, continuity, integration, navigation, and variety within the design.

hierarchical development

Hierarchy depends on the complementing and contrasting relationships of visual elements. It is established by creating a clear focal point that attracts the eye to initiate viewer interaction with the design. Supporting the focal point, the melding of subordinate visual elements allows for in-depth analysis, interpretation, and understanding. When dominant and subordinate elements coalesce, the design maintains the fixed attention of the eye. The viewer begins to recognize the ordering system and is led through a logical and meaningful journey. If the visual elements demand equal attention, the eye is distracted and moves continuously around the surface of the page without direction. This type of design lacks impact, legibility, and usefulness. Nothing is communicated, and the result is a visual muddle.

Revealing messages through an integrated hierarchy is an effective approach to organizing content and enhancing the value of the design. Hierarchy is inherent to the comprehensive function of the design whether it is simple or complex, conservative or expressive, quiet or loud. Developed and controlled by the designer, a methodical system synthesizes the design.

| *design* philippe archontakis | *A striking color palette commands the letterhead system for Bleu+Associés. Eye-catching fields of blue, white, and orange lead the viewer toward the typographic content. The typography is quietly composed near the edges of the page, with negative space and tension providing emphasis.*

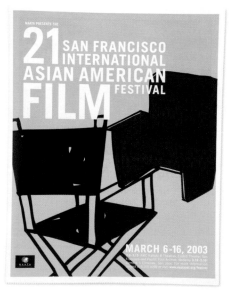

| *design* noon | *This booklet cover uses clean typography and colorful illustration for visual impact. The typographic focal point is positioned in the top-left corner. The uppercase setting is commanding, and multiple type sizes express levels of importance within the cluster of text. The design flows horizontally downward, through the illustration, to reveal secondary messages resting in the bottom-right corner.*

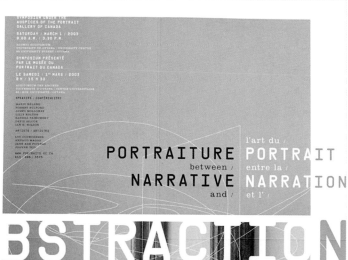

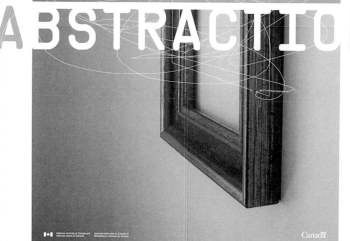

| **design** kolégram | *The hierarchic structure of this poster is dictated by its centrally located title, Abstraction. Providing initial impact, the title divides the design into halves, which connotes the contrast between abstraction and reality. The subtitle, set in English and French, remains proximate to the title, yet distinct, in a smaller type size. The tertiary text sits modestly in the top-left corner.*

| **design** renate gokl | *This invitation opens horizontally and vertically— the viewer can choose either side of the piece to experience first. Both orientations present an open, structured design that demonstrates hierarchy through typographic variation. Using a single typeface— Bell Gothic—adjustments in type size, weight, and color differentiate dominant and subordinate content.*

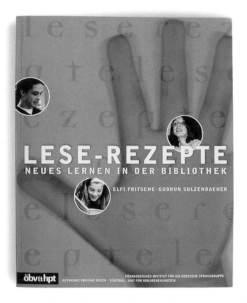

Die Titelredaktion

Texte in Sachbüchern lassen sich leichter lesen und verstehen, wenn sie strukturiert sind.

Sachtexte sind nicht immer leicht verständlich. Oft fehlt erklärendes Bildmaterial, oft ist der Text kompliziert und kaum gegliedert. Präsentiert sich eine Buchseite sobetrachtet, wird das Buch häufig weggelegt.

Es gibt einfache, doch umso wirkungsvollere Wege, die einen Text für den jugendlichen Leser interessant machen. Eines dieser Mittel ist der Zwischentitel.

Als Redakteure erfahren die Schüler, wie Autoren ihre Leser motivieren und ihren Stoff verständlich machen. Sie untersuchen Zwischentitel und versuchen, selber welche zu finden. Sie lernen die Variationsmöglichkeiten bei Zwischentiteln kennen und anwenden.

Bei Redaktionsschluss rauchen die Köpfe, und alle wundern sich, wie viele neue Informationen in kurzer Zeit erfasst und vielfältig gestaltet geworden sind.

Zubereitung

Die Lehrerin präsentiert der Klasse zwei aufgeschlagene Sachbücher: Die Doppelseite des einen Buches zeigt einen strukturierten Text mit mehreren, leicht lesbaren Zwischentiteln. „Uns interessieren an diesen beiden Sachbüchern nicht die Bilder, sondern der Text, Was fällt euch auf der ersten Blick auf?" Je nach Altersstufe gibt die Lehrerin Artikulationshilfen: „Wie sieht hier der Text aus? Ist er eingeteilt? Gibt es Absätze? Haben die Absätze Überschriften?"

Nach dieser ersten kurzen Gesprächsrunde gehen die Schüler zu einem Tisch mit Sachbüchern. Zu zweit sollen sie nun zwei Bücher austauschen und entscheiden, ob die Texte darin im Block oder in Bausteinen gestaltet sind. Eine Sache von fünf Minuten.

Dann schlagen sie bei beiden Büchern je eine ausgewählte Doppelseite auf und legen die Bücher auf den Boden, entweder zur Karte „Fließtext" oder zur Karte „strukturierter Text".

→

Zutaten

- 30 Sachbücher, die Hälfte davon mit strukturiertem Text
- Zwei Karten: „Fließtext" und „strukturierter Text"
- Schreibzeug
- Eineinhalb Stunden Zeit

---

design no.parking — The image of the hand creates a strong visual impression. Although it fills the cover, it does not dominate the composition. The reduced value of the image contrasts with the white title treatment, which elevates the typography to the focal point. In addition, the use of subordinate, textural type in the middle ground of the design adds depth.

| *design* no.parking | An interior spread features changes in typographic scale and weight to denote the textual hierarchy of the design. A colored, rectangular shape breaks the monotony of the white page and interrupts the horizontal motion of the typography. The contrast in orientation effectively leads the eye across and down the page to access all content.

Hierarchical development begins by ranking the visual elements by importance. Simply, the designer must determine what he or she wants the viewer to see first, second, third, and so on. By giving the visual elements an order, or level of importance, the designer defines the role each element will play in the delivery of the message. Dominant elements will reside in the foreground and demand attention, whereas subordinate elements will activate the middle ground or background in support of the dominant elements. For example, on the chapter title spreads in this book, the titles dominate the page—they are the primary focal point. In support, graphic shapes and linear elements punctuate the compositional space, and additional text, including subtitles, body copy, and page numbers, are subordinate to the titles. Every element is carefully considered because their roles are critical in effectively shaping the page.

Initial hierarchical considerations also include determining which visual elements are the same (or closely related to each other). The designer groups the elements to forge consistency and visual relationships throughout the design. For example, the designer groups together all headings or body copy. When the layout of the visual elements begins, the content is already dissected and prepared in groups for use. It is clearly defined at the beginning of the design process which elements are partnered. During the design phase, the designer must establish the strongest visual treatment for each group and apply it universally throughout the design. Once the viewer recognizes the repeated treatments, comprehension is enabled—the viewer is aware of the ordering system and can easily access primary, secondary, and tertiary information.

compositional factors

The designer works with compositional factors to achieve hierarchy throughout the layout. The harmonious integration of multiple factors plays a critical role when shaping the page. The designer must experiment and determine which factors effectively contribute to and define the ordered presentation of textual and visual information.

compositional factors

contrast   position

orientation   color

scale   graphic shapes

quantity   dimension

linear elements   tension

depth   typography

perspective   space

                      repetition

When the visual elements have been ranked and grouped, the design process can begin. To continue developing a strong, hierarchical system, the designer must activate the compositional factors and create visual contrast. Some compositional factors include space, scale, and quantity as well as orientation and dimension. Although each individual factor can be manipulated to achieve contrast, the designer must decide which are most useful and coordinate their interaction within the design.

The designer must thoughtfully control and finesse the compositional factors to avoid monotonous or overactive visual fields. Monotony will ensue if all elements share equal importance and visual strength. The design will lack hierarchy, and it will be impossible for the viewer to determine the most important content from the least significant. On the other hand, if the design is overactive, the visual elements will compete for attention. Although the composition may make a strong first impression, it will be too energetic and lack function and will not provide a starting point to engage the viewer. The designer must remember that all elements cannot be visually equal.

Contrast is the essential factor needed to achieve successful hierarchy within the design. It effectively distinguishes all the visual elements that interact in the compositional space. By creating visual differences, juxtaposed elements efficiently communicate their intended meaning. The visual contrast that exists between the elements makes them identifiable and comprehensible to the viewer, who notes the differences and deciphers the dominant and subordinate levels of information. Decisive contrast between disparate visual elements makes the hierarchical system visually apparent and the design effectively communicates its intended messages in a logical progression.

space Space is an important compositional factor that the designer must consider. If used competently, space provides visual contrast and contributes to an effective ordering system. The empty compositional space brings the visual elements alive; it is the invisible energy of the design and must be considered a dominant element. The designer must focus attention toward the activity (or inactivity) of the negative space to activate the visual elements that reside within it. Space is needed in all compositions—it is imperative to accessibility and navigation. It provides pathways, or channels, that lead the eye through the design, while directing the visual focus toward the positive areas of the compositional space.

The designer can take advantage of space in several ways. On a simple level, visual elements can be grouped together by limiting the amount of space between them to create a focal point. Increasing space between elements separates them. The extra space leads the eye to the isolated elements. In other cases, space affects the visual elements based on their position. For example, centering a visual element in the middle of the page equalizes the space around it, rendering the space ineffective. On the other hand, positioning a visual element to the right or left of center, as well as near the top or bottom of the page, creates weighted, asymmetric space. For example, if a larger amount of space is on the bottom of the composition and the visual elements rise to the top or above the optical center of the page, the design feels grounded. Space secures the element in place.

Excessive amounts of space that are used ineffectively do not activate the page because the visual elements fade into the background, and space dominates. If the amount of negative space is limited because the design is overfilled, it is unclear for the viewer how to navigate through the design in a logical progression. The visual elements are trapped within the edges of the page, and the design does not deliver its message.

| *design* kearneyrocholl | *Delicate rectangular shapes frame the body text of this catalogue. Their pale hues make them barely apparent, and they recede into the background. In addition, large headings, set in the typeface Nya, effectively direct the eye. Three decisive type sizes indicate primary, secondary, and tertiary text, whereas color changes provide additional contrast.*

| *design* kearneyrocholl | *A text-heavy page significantly contrasts with its facing page, which is light and open. The balance created between the pages, as well as the use of large numbers, makes the design accessible.*

scale Scale relationships produce immediate contrast. If the visual elements demonstrate changes in scale, both large and small, the contrast between them establishes an adequate hierarchy. If all the elements are the same size or visual weight, they will negate the hierarchical force of each other. The compositional field is optically even and lacks a decisive focal point. Each element demands the same amount of attention and nothing is subordinate.

When adjusting the scale of the visual elements, the designer must use consistency and progression. Randomly changing scale is inadequate and leads to chaos because nothing is related. It is important that all scale changes be considered in relationship to every element of the composition. A clear, hierarchical distinction exists between small, medium, and large visual elements, and progressive scale variations also give the design rhythm. Varying scale relationships defines the appropriate, logical order of the visual elements while improving navigation through the design.

OASIS WINES

2001

OASIS
Pinot Noir

ALC 12% BY VOL

Produced and bottled in Santa Maria, California

FOR MORE INFORMATION ABOUT THIS WINE FOR MORE INFORMATION FOR MORE INFORMATION ABOUT THIS WINE FOR MORE INFORMATION ABOUT THIS WINE FOR MORE INFORMATION ABOUT THIS WINE FOR MORE INFORMATION ABOUT THIS WINE FOR MORE

| *design* ingalls + associates |
The contrast between typographic elements establishes the hierarchy of the Oasis wine label. Changes in scale produce immediate contrast; the largest element is the most dominant. To increase the visual differences, a bold, sans serif title complements and contrasts with the subtitle, which is set in a fluid script.

Jordan Crane balanziert zwischen Photographie und Kunst mit ähnlichem Enthusiasmus. Neben einer langen Liste von hochprofessioneller kommerzieller Arbeit und einem MFA von der Cornell Universität wurden seine Arbeit in einer Reihe bekannter Gallerien ausgestellt. Jordan Crane (31) lebt in Lamertville, New Jersey einer kleinen Stadt am Delaware River.

crispy clicks

| *design* kearneyrocholl | The quantity of visual information on the spread is plentiful, and progressive changes in the size of the photographs create depth. The negative space complements the rectilinear layout because it is proportionately related to the size and shape of the imagery. Clear spatial pathways lead the eye through the composition.

the interaction of visual elements

quantity The quantity of elements also affects the designer's ability to produce effective visual contrast and hierarchy. Incorporating unnecessary visual elements beyond the project requirements can result in visual clutter and a lack of order. The designer must be cautious not to add unnecessary imagery, graphic shapes, or linear elements unless they have a specific function. For example, if too many elements (no matter how subordinate) are present in the design, they will confuse the order of the presentation. In this case, it is helpful to reduce the visual elements to the bare essentials. Carefully editing or eliminating information, a subtractive method, adds clarity and impact. Although additional elements are beneficial in some cases, the designer must always remember that excessive visual noise, in addition to the required elements of the design, can distract the viewer and negate the ordering system.

Counter to subtractive methods, the designer may choose to intentionally increase the quantity of visual elements on the page—an additive method—to enhance the delivery of the message. The added elements, which can include graphic shapes and linear elements, add visual impact and variation to the required elements of the design. For example, a graphic shape or linear element that directs the eye toward the dominant text effectively strengthens hierarchy. It can be a positive addition to the design without adding visual noise. Additional elements that are incorporated into the design must reinforce or support the primary message. Every design project differs, and the designer must attain balance and learn when to appropriately add or edit information to benefit the communicative function of the design.

| *design* enspace | The angular orientation of the visual elements enlivens this poster. The inverted position of the conductor provides immediate visual impact—it is a decisive focal point. Intentional shifts in the orientation and color activate the design. Each element plays off the other to forge solid relationships.

| *design* helicopter | The limited space on the clear inlay of this CD packaging does not negate an effective hierarchy. The composition moves out from the center, which is the focal point. Beginning with the title of the album and name of the performer, the content progresses from dominate to subordinate. Linear elements divide the circle and provide equal spatial intervals for typography.

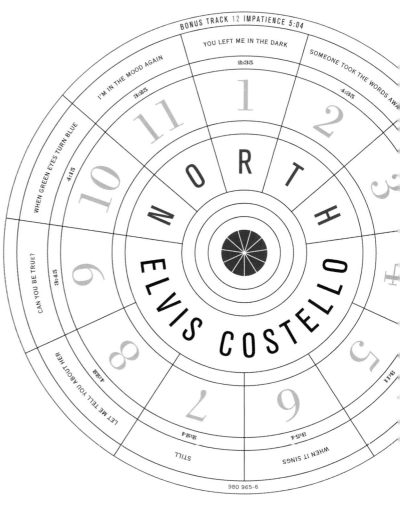

orientation and position Orientation and position are additional factors that foster contrast and distinctive hierarchy. When composing the page, the designer positions the visual elements throughout the design along the top, bottom, and sides of the page as clustered groups or isolated elements in horizontal, vertical, or diagonal orientations. Shifting orientation and position of visual elements is an effective way to command attention. For example, if all the elements are horizontally oriented, a strong vertical element draws attention. Or, if a composition is composed along a diagonal axis, rotating one or a series of elements at an opposing angle effectively leads the viewer to that distinct area of the design. (Diagonals are dynamic and directly contrast the rectilinear shape of the page. They add immediate drama and movement.) In addition, the intersection points of horizontal, vertical, and diagonal elements are active, providing focal points by leading the eye to the area where all the elements meet. Positioning visual elements near the edge or running off the page creates visual tension, which also draws the viewer toward specific areas of the composition.

| *design* **helicopter** | *An interior spread of the CD booklet demonstrates control over a large number of textual elements. The spread contains song titles, production information, and lyrics in four languages. Despite the quantity of information, the layout is clear and ordered. Linear elements are added to enhance the structure of the design.*

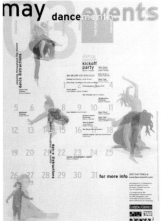

| *design* **visual dialogue** | *Layered, repeated photography commands attention, scale provides impact and movement, and transparency and value add depth. The photography is also directional; note how the bent knee of the figure points toward the starting point of the typography on the front of the design. Changes in typographic scale, as well as orientation and position, define the organization of the text.*

depth, dimension, and perspective

Perspective is a unique way to engage the compositional space of the page while contrasting and distinguishing visual elements. The use of perspective shifts the two-dimensional surface of the design into the third dimension—depth is created, and the compositional field is extended. Elements positioned in perspective recede or move out toward the viewer. In addition, the implied lines moving toward vanishing points are directive and lead the eye toward visual elements positioned along that distinctive line. (Use perspective carefully. Be cautious and avoid skewing imagery or typography in an inappropriate way that alters its character or integrity.)

Layering visual elements also helps achieve depth and dimension on the page. The designer can take advantage of foreground, middle ground, and background to expand the visual environment of the composition. Also, primary, secondary, and tertiary levels of importance can be easily organized in the foreground, middle ground, and background areas of the composition. Repetition creates depth and dimension as well as rhythm throughout the design while emphasizing the specific visual elements that are repeated. In addition, patterns and textures can be used to draw attention or create interest in specific areas of the composition.

| *design* nb: studio | A conservative, yet well-considered, hierarchical structure is demonstrated in the typographic system of this catalogue. The order of the text is distinguished by changes in typeface, as well as size, weight, and color. A blue heading calls immediate attention at the top of the page. The space between the heading and the body copy reinforces its dominant hierarchy.

| *design* kristin cullen | This poster demonstrates compositional depth, whereas the use of scale and perspective leads the viewer in a logical order. The typographic treatment is contrasted by organic imagery and provides the starting point for entry into the design. Multiple vanishing points create dimension and enhance the space of the page.

typography Like all considerations throughout the design process, typographic application needs careful attention and consistent application to be effective and contribute to the hierarchical system. Initially, the text needs to be broken into levels of importance and then purposefully set to visually distinguish all typographic variables and clarify their order of presentation. The designer's goal is to create consistency with enough visual contrast that the viewer can discern the typographic differences and access the content efficiently. A uniformly applied system allows the viewer to make visual connections. For example, the consistent treatment of headings enables the viewer to recognize easily the typographic organization because of its repetitious treatment.

Innumerable options for distinguishing one level of typographic information from the next are available. A simple method to achieve contrast and emphasis is changing the type size. However, changes in size are often predictable, and other methods of contrast and emphasis are sometimes more desirable, especially in text-heavy compositions. (Too many changes in type size can be confusing and can lead to disorder.) When considering alternative options to scale changes, the designer can use italic (also oblique) or bold styles of a single typeface to create emphasis within limited quantities of textual content. Also, areas of text that demand attention can be set in full or small capitals, as well as lowercase settings. A broad typeface family with diverse styles, weights, and widths will provide a range of visual options, including condensed and extended typefaces. Combinations of serif and sans serif typefaces are also distinctive and provide effective contrast, if used together competently. The designer must explore the possibilities and discover the range of available choices.

for in-depth typographic information, refer to chapter 7: typography shaping the page

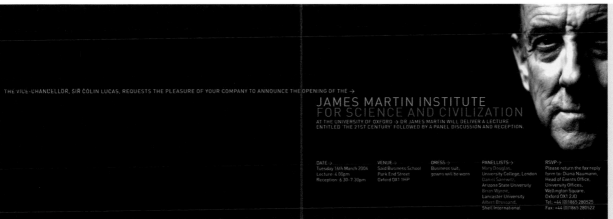

| ***design*** wilsonharvey/loewy |

Mimicking the yellow rule on the cover, a single line of typography leads the eye across the interior spread toward the dominant area of the design. Typographic color and scale effectively call attention to James Martin Institute. It is surrounded by dramatic negative space, which is the backbone of the composition.

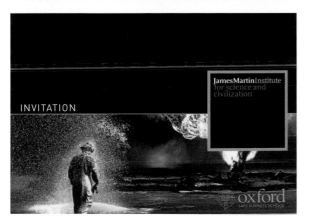

| ***design*** wilsonharvey/loewy |

The word invitation *is visually dominant because of not only its isolated position on the left side of the page but the stark contrast of white type on a black field— it equals the weight of the photograph below. A yellow linear element reinforces the baseline of the text and leads the viewer across the page.*

the interaction of visual elements

color Color is a useful compositional factor that provides visual interest and emphasizes specific elements of the design. It can be added to graphic shapes and linear elements as well as typographic content. Color can also be used to fill large fields to create rich backgrounds, or it can be used to isolate select areas of the design that need attention. For example, color can be applied to all the headings to make them identifiable. Or, a colored bar can surround the headings; this technique also effectively distinguishes the content. Careful consideration of color and its balance on the page is a critical component of the design process. The designer can establish a comprehensive color palette or use only one or two colors. Often, the designer works with several colors to test the hues that evoke the best overall impression and lead the viewer through the design effectively.

| *design* the jones group | Interior spreads feature bright, warm colors that activate the foreground. Yellow text rises to the surface of the page, and the effect is appropriate for the large headings Imagine and Your Peace of Mind. Graphic shapes and linear elements also support the design. Notably, a star accents the center of an image, drawing attention toward shaking hands, which reinforces the image's message.

| *design* the jones group | Bands of color create a bright field and direct the eye down the cover toward descriptive text. They also provide alignment points for typography. The smallest piece of text commands visual attention because it is the only element within a field of color. Its separation makes it distinctive.

By adjusting the color of the visual elements, the designer can reinforce content and heighten its meaning. He or she must consider the tone of the design and use colors that complement or contrast the attitude of the piece. For example, red connotes heat, passion, and urgency, whereas blue is cool and quiet. Warm colors (red, orange, and yellow) rise to the surface of the composition and effectively command attention. Cool colors (green, blue, and purple) recede; their quiet impression is evident but often secondary to warmer colors. Even if using one color, the designer can create impressions of depth using value. Whereas darker values move to the foreground, lighter values recede in a monochromatic composition. In addition, pairing contrasting colors draws the eye toward specific sections of the composition. Bright and saturated colors will have immediate impact, if used sparingly. If everything is bright or heavily saturated, the composition will lack focus. Experimentation will help the designer understand the effectiveness of color and its impact on hierarchy.

| design creative inc. | Photography provides visual impact, and color directs the viewer toward important content. Bright pink commands the foreground and emphasizes select text. It also accents graphic shapes, including arrows that are directed toward important content. The text, which is subordinate to the imagery, is minimal in setting and allows the photography to drive the message.

graphic shapes and linear elements Graphic shapes and linear elements are added to the composition to create dynamic visual fields, support the primary content, and direct the viewer toward the important areas. Both graphic shapes and linear elements are directional tools. If used effectively, they aid navigation and prevent the design from becoming static. The designer uses graphic shapes and linear elements to create movement throughout the design. These elements provide the skeletal framework for the position of and passage toward the positive areas of the design.

A bold, graphic shape can provide the background of the composition while also serving as carriers for illustrations, photography, or typographic elements. In addition to graphic shapes, linear elements also function in countless ways. For example, rules can frame pieces of texts or provide baselines for typographic elements to sit on or rise above and below, thereby grounding the typography. Rules can also be applied to reinforce the structure of the composition and direct the eye toward the visual elements that align along the edges of spatial intervals.

| *design* 33rpm | *A subtle image of a landscape establishes the foreground of this poster. Although the typographic content lies in the background, it is still the dominant visual element. The white lettering strongly contrasts with the dark, solid field and commands attention. The typography also demonstrates a scale progression, which effectively orders the text.*

| *design* patent pending | *Organic graphic shapes provide ground, as well as direction, in this set of posters. In the first poster, the directional thrust of the conical shapes emphasizes the repetitious title treatment. In the second poster, organic shapes are introduced and provide an immediate visual impression that leads the eye into the design toward to centrally composed lettering.*

photography abelardo morell, camera obscura image of la girardita de la habana in room with broken wall, 2000

| *design* collaborated inc. | *This invitation is simply executed with clear hierarchy. Changes in scale and value easily distinguish the text. On the back of the piece, the ordering of text is accessible, moving from the top to the bottom of the page in progressive sizes.*

out of place fundraiser

hosted by
lucy aptekar and bernie toale
thursday november 13 2003
6–8pm

at the home of lucy aptekar
38 cumberland avenue brookline ma 02445
stop caps from the work in progress and enjoy hors
hors d'oeuvres and refreshments

rsvp by november 3
allie hunsenok 617 876 0013 or allishum3@mac.com

FINAL THOUGHTS Hierarchy is critical to the appropriateness and effectiveness of the visual solution. Without it, the design lacks purpose, and the communicative function is lost. The designer must order and control the design, using contrast to establish the visual levels of dominance and subordination. Using compositional forces, including color, graphic shapes, and linear elements, effectively and with purpose, the designer will be able to integrate all the elements harmoniously. However, it is important to remember that some elements will lead the design, whereas others should intentionally follow.

| *design* kf design | *The position of the photograph faces into the composition rather than out of it. The doll directs the eye toward the caption at the bottom of the page. A horizontal graphic shape runs across the spread, which contains and grounds the title within the spacious environment. In addition, the contrast of the white type on the black background brings the title to the foreground.*

Good type is good

because it has natural strength and beauty.

The best results come, as a rule,

from finding the best type for the work

and then guiding it

with the gentlest possible hand.

ROBERT BRINGHURST

author, book designer, historian, poet, teacher, typographer

TYPOGRAPHY

SHAPING THE PAGE

Typography is visible language. Representing human thoughts, it fosters exchange and preserves intellect through sight, speech, and sound. It is the foundation of visual communication. Typography delivers an array of information from insignificant memos to life-sustaining facts that is essential to daily function and understanding. It is beautiful and ugly, engaging and irritating, meaningful and trivial. Indelibly linked to everyday experience, it is ubiquitous. Typography enlivens communication. It is a voice that resonates on the surface of the page, setting the tone of the design.

the function of type

typographic characteristics

Typography unifies the design through its complementing and contrasting juxtaposition with all the visual elements. The designer composes type to invite the viewer into and cultivate their relationship with the design. A decisive, well-planned system encourages readability and comprehension. Type is the leading factor (the conductor of the orchestra) that controls the activity of the page (the symphony) and enables sequential flow. Nurturing order and structural harmony, typography aesthetically invigorates text with meaning. It is the framework for the exchange of ideas from one person to another.

Designing with type is an artful, detail-oriented activity that demands competence and patience. Nothing can be overlooked, from the overall composition to its subtleties. Whether type exists as letters, words, lines, and paragraphs, or image, texture, and graphic form, typographic expression is unlimited. Any text, in any form and environment, can be made meaningful through intelligent application. Working with typography is a delicate balance of understanding and intuition, conformity and rebellion. The designer is limited only by his or her imagination.

| *design* hendersonbromsteadartco. | *This poster is a successful union of expressive lettering and illustration. Creating visual impact from a distance, the design incites interaction. Hand-drawn letterforms replicate the shape of a scarf and change orientation and scale to encourage readability.*

| *design* no.parking | *The cover and title page of* di(e)verse, *a book of poetry, presents a subtle shift in the baseline that drops the (e) from alignment with the rest of the title. In addition, the x-height of the title is used to position the authors' names in a vertical orientation.*

Typefaces have personalities—cold, sophisticated, or friendly—which establish the attitude of the design. They provide an immediate first impression that is critical to the delivery of messages. Type engages (or disengages) the viewer. Typefaces must possess the proper character to connote the spirit of the design while practically supporting legibility and readability. It is a constant rule that the function, content, and end user define the typeface selection process. If typefaces are chosen carelessly, they will not serve the communicative function of the design. It is not a process to be overlooked or considered lightly.

classification Classification systems organize typefaces into similar groupings that allow for identification based on unifying characteristics. Typefaces can be broken down into five main classifications: Old Style, Transitional, Modern, Slab Serif, and Sans Serif. Display and Script classifications account for decorative typefaces that do not fit elsewhere. In most applications, typefaces are chosen from the five classifications. (The designer may also consider handcrafted or computer-generated methods of creating letterforms, which provide a distinctive style to the design.)

Old Style
bembo

Transitional
baskerville

Modern
bodoni

Slab Serif
clarendon

Sans Serif
trade gothic

Display
cooper black

Script
zapf chancery

Typefaces are organized into different classifications according to their unifying characteristics, including stroke weight, serif or sans serif style, and vertical stress, or axis, of rounded forms.

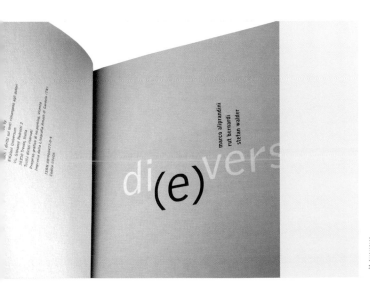

| design no.parking | *An interior spread provides alternative settings for the poetry. Contrast between the open, gridded letterforms (verso) and dense, justified paragraph (recto) adds typographic color to the stable composition.*

style, weight, and width The style of a typeface indicates if it is regular (also roman), italic (also oblique), or bold. Italic and bold fonts are necessities when working with type. They can be used to achieve contrast and provide emphasis because of the shift in appearance from the regular style, as well as their lighter or darker impressions on the page. However, large amounts of italic and bold text are less readable than their regular counterparts. Also, when using italic and bold styles, always select the font from within the typeface family that is used. Do not rely on computer-generated italic and bold styles—they are merely sloped or thickened. True italic and bold fonts are considered in the design of the type family. For example, italic fonts often have linked characters, whereas bold faces have adapted counters to accommodate heavier stroke widths.

Weight refers to the lightness or darkness of letterforms marked by a change in stroke width. It is indicated by terms such as light, medium, bold, heavy, and black. Width refers to different variations within a typeface family, such as condensed, compressed, or extended fonts. Contributing to the typographic color of the page, changes in type weight and width add depth and variety. They also are used to differentiate information, which helps order the text.

x-height and cap height X-height refers to the height of the lowercase letters without ascenders and descenders. Ascenders rise up from the baseline above the x-height to the cap height and sometimes higher. Descenders fall below the baseline. X-height is easily determined by looking at the lowercase x. Cap height refers to the height of the capital letters, measured from the baseline (the line on which the letters sit) to the capline (the line at the top of uppercase letters). Because the x-height and cap height vary with each typeface, it is useful to compare them when combining typefaces.

counters Counters are white spaces located inside of and around letterforms that affect legibility, readability, and density of typefaces. Counter space varies with each font, depending on its size, height, weight, and width. For example, thin fonts used at large type sizes have open counters that can overpower the light strokes, but bold fonts often need more room between each letter to compensate for the diminished counters.

small capitals SMALL CAPITALS are complete sets of uppercase letters that are the same height as lowercase letters. They can be used when capitals, such as acronyms or abbreviations, appear within normal text. Replacing FULL CAPITALS, SMALL CAPITALS avoid unwanted emphasis that FULL CAPITALS command because of their larger appearance. SMALL CAPITALS allow the text to flow without interruption. Additionally, they can be used to call out specific parts of the text, like subheads, headers, or footers. They are typically featured in serif typefaces, although many contemporary sans serif typefaces, such as Meta or Finnegan, include SMALL CAPITAL fonts.

35 Light	55 Roman	**85 Heavy Oblique**
35 Light Oblique	*55 Oblique*	**85 Heavy**
45 Book	65 Medium	**95 Black**
45 Book Oblique	*65 Medium Oblique*	***95 Black Oblique***

Avenir, designed by Adrian Frutiger, is a contemporary sans serif typeface with a number of styles and weights. A diverse typeface provides a range of options that adds depth and variety to compositions.

ascender

capline

cap height

meanline

x-height

baseline

full capital   small capital   counter

descender

Basic terms, including baseline, capline, x-height, ascender, descender, and counter, are used consistently in the designer's vocabulary. Understanding the structural components of typography is inherent to designing with it effectively.

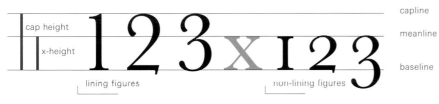

capline

cap height

meanline

x-height

baseline

lining figures   non-lining figures

Lining and non-lining figures are two types of numerals available in many typefaces. Lining figures are the same size as capitals letters, whereas non-lining figures, also known as old style, are the same x-height as lowercase letters.

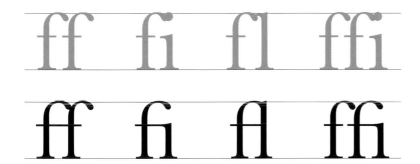

Replacing letters that collide when paired together, ligatures are unique characters produced by combining two or three letters into one cohesive form.

lining and non-lining figures Typefaces have one or two sets of numerals. The first set is lining figures, which are the same height and width as full capitals. They work well in combination with uppercase letters, as well as for tabular information that requires the precise alignment of numerals. However, lining figures can be too large in many text settings. For example, if they will be used in sequence with lowercase letters, optically match their sizes to avoid unnecessary emphasis. Reducing the type size of the lining numerals by one point usually will suffice.

The second set of numerals is non-lining figures, also known as old style. They share the same x-height as the lowercase letters and feature ascenders, descenders, and variable widths. Old style numerals fit comfortably within continuous text, eliminating unwanted attention that interferes with readability. They work well with small capitals but will appear too small next to full capitals. Old style numerals connote refinement compared to solid lining figures. Although not all typefaces have old style numerals, they are common in serif and some sans serif typefaces. It is advantageous to select typefaces with both sets of numerals to have the broadest range of typographic options.

ligatures A ligature is a specially designed character produced by combining two or three letters into one unified form. Ligatures replace pairs of letters that collide into each other to improve legibility. In many typefaces, the lowercase *f* extends into the space of the letter following it. If that letter rises above the x-height, it will touch the *f*. Common ligatures include ff, ffi, ffl, fi, and fj. Like old style numerals and small capitals, not all typefaces have ligatures (or need them). If they are included in the character set, it makes sense to use them.

typeface selection

With an understanding of the characteristics of typefaces, the selection process begins. The first step is to evaluate the purpose and longevity of the design. Is it a book that will sit on a shelf for years? Is it a brochure for a one-time event that will cease to function afterward? Is the design geared toward a broad or specific audience? Once the function of the design is determined, select a range of serif and sans serif type families, as well as display faces, considering historical and contemporary connotations. (Typefaces that are innovative one year might be appropriate and timely, or they could be outdated. Traditional faces that go beyond fashion could be classic and timeless, or they could be too conservative.) Examine the full type family in a variety of settings that match the requirements of the design. To help narrow the options, compare the selections side by side and determine which evoke favored emotions, demonstrate maximum legibility and readability, and reflect the needs of the client and viewer.

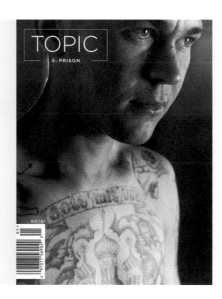

| *design* giampietro+smith |

The typeface Gotham is set in a range of weights and establishes hierarchy and color. The combination of fonts, as well as upper- and lowercase settings, distinguishes author names, articles, and descriptions. Gotham features a tall x-height with spacious counters that enhance readability and add white space to the page.

| *design* giampietro+smith |

An image-based cover with a subtle typographic title, Topic, establishes the mood of the magazine. The clean presentation of the uppercase setting alludes to the design that lies within.

When selecting typefaces, analyze the number of words, as well as the different kinds of textual content. As the design grows in complexity, more typographic options are needed to differentiate the levels of information. Position, scale, and orientation are effective methods to establish typographic hierarchy without a change in style (regular, italic, and bold) or typeface; however, this is also limiting. For example, a typical spread from this book contains headings, subheadings, body text, captions, headers, footers, and folios. This is a considerable number of variables that need individual attention in relationship to the whole. Their diversity dictates the need for a flexible, reliable typeface family with full character sets (alphabet, numerals, punctuation, and diacritics) and a range of fonts. Fonts include styles (regular, italic, and bold), weights (light, medium, bold, heavy, and black), and widths (condensed or extended).

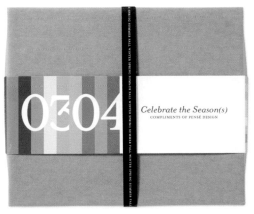

| *design* pensé design | *This packaging features one typeface, Mrs Eaves. It is applied with a range of settings, including lining numerals, italics, and capitals. Hierarchy is achieved through the use of contrast and scale. The design demonstrates that a single typeface family can effectively provide variety.*

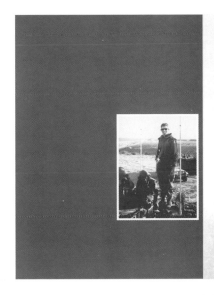

| *design* giampietro+smith |
Interior spreads introduce the serif typeface Miller, which harmoniously contrasts with the sans serif Gotham. Used for subheadings and justified body text, Miller contrasts nicely with the light letterforms and darkens the page with its strong, heavy characteristics.

| *design* giampietro+smith |
A close-up details the centered alignment of text that is simply set and readable. Its quiet presentation is subordinate to the black-and-white photograph on which it rests. Note the use of the fi ligature in the word crucified on the first line.

combining typefaces A single type family with a range of fonts will satisfy the needs of any project. However, for a broader typographic palette, the designer should also investigate combining typefaces. Multiple type families, typically up to two or three, extend the typographic possibilities within the design. Not only do they provide visual contrast, they also help the designer establish hierarchy by distinguishing information. Additional typefaces can enhance typographic color, rhythm, and texture while adding perceived value and sophistication to the design.

Typefaces are often combined based on their comparative visual characteristics. For example, serif and sans serif typefaces with similar widths and x-heights, such as Sabon and Syntax, are comfortable pairings. Type families that have been designed by a single designer and share proportional relationships are strong matches. A harmonious combination is Meridien and Frutiger designed by Adrian Frutiger. Some typefaces, such as Rotis and Thesis, are designed with sans serif, semi sans, and serif variations that are consistently designed throughout the extensive family.

In addition, two serifs or sans serifs with considerable visual differences may be paired together. They should be notably distinct to provide enough contrast to justify the combination. If the pairing is too similar, it will look like a mistake, rather than an intentional decision. Bodoni and Didot or Helvetica and Akzidenz Grotesque are examples of poor combinations due to their marked similarities. Finally, do not forget about display and script typefaces that can add unique style to the treatment of limited information, such as titles, headings, subheadings, or folios (never use to set continuous text). Display and script faces suitably combine with serif and sans serif typefaces.

All typefaces merit the designer's respect and attention. No matter what is used, never intentionally stretch, expand, or condense letterforms. They are designed with specific proportions for optimal settings. Wrongly skewing type destroys the integrity of the typeface, as well as the intentions of the type designer. If it is not the perfect fit, find another typeface that has the desired characteristics. This is an easy solution, considering the number of typefaces available to the designer.

| *design* concrete [the office of jilly simons] | *This announcement for Hinge, a sound studio, reveals information through transparent sheets. The layout relies on typography to carry the message and bring the viewer into the design. Layers of letters and numbers create intrigue by sharing a consistent baseline that cohesively blends the pages together.*

10years

10,000 sessions eep

Thesis
TheSans
TheMix
TheSerif

Several contemporary typefaces, including Rotis and Thesis, include sans serif, semi sans, semi serif, and serif variations, which share similar proportions throughout the family and provide multiple typographic options.

Rotis
Sans Serif
Semi Sans Serif
Semi Serif
Serif

Sabon
Syntax
Meridien
Frutiger

An examination of the characteristics of letterforms, such as comparable widths and x-heights, is an important step in selecting serif and sans serif typeface combinations, including Sabon and Syntax. In addition, typefaces that share proportional relationships and are designed by one designer often combine well, such as Meridien and Frutiger by Adrian Frutiger.

Bodoni
Didot
Grotesque
Helvetica

Typefaces that fall within the same classification share comparable features and often result in poor combinations because of their notable resemblance and lack of visual contrast.

a sound studio

HINGE

320 West Ohio Street Chicago Illinois

info@hingestudios.com

TELE 312 337 0008

| *design* concrete [the office of jilly simons] | *On the fourth spread, typefaces change to surprise the viewer and contrast the tone of the previously seen condensed face. The design loosens up with the energy brought to the page through the arrangement and combination of typefaces.*

designing with type

It is critical for the designer to be intimately familiar with the text before working with it. Every project is unique and demands different approaches based on the content. Determining the function of the design before shaping the page influences its typographic presentation. Is it an annual report that contains several charts and lists that demand easy access? Is it a poster with limited textual content that needs visual impact? Is it a book with large amounts of continuous text? The designer composes and controls typography to lead the viewer through the design without visual roadblocks that prevent accessibility and comprehension.

Confidence won through performance

DEDICATED TO EARNING YOUR TRUST

In an ideal world, there would be no worry about financial affairs. Unfortunately, the world is not ideal. Burlwood Financial aims to ease your concerns about financial matters through performance, integrity and service excellence. We look to forge a partnership with you based on unshakable trust.

PEACE OF MIND Trust can be promised. To take root, however, it must be earned.

At Burlwood, our promise is to work diligently to earn your trust. We recognize the enormity of the responsibility you place with us. Our pledge is never to take it lightly.

To earn your trust, we must demonstrate performance, commitment and sensitivity. We must work to deepen our understanding of your needs and goals through regular communication.

In addition, we must demonstrate that your interests have priority over all others—especially our own. In this, we must be above reproach. Our advice to you must be unbiased, not based on prospects of our own personal gain. To that end, we have adopted a fee structure that directly aligns our incentives with your goals.

We would welcome the opportunity to begin a relationship in which trust takes root and grows. For us, there is no greater achievement than such a relationship.

Our aim is to serve a small group of clients, to know them intimately and to gain their trust. Our first step is to identify their goals. Only when it is clear what they want to accomplish and a plan is in place do we invest their money and navigate the risks.

| *design* capsule | *One typeface demonstrates shifts in scale and position to achieve an ordered design. Large type commands presence without cluttering the layout, which features a strong horizontal grid line from which the primary text hangs. Subordinate typographic information is set in smaller sizes that progressively move across the page; their position and amount of text determine their importance.*

legibility and readability Legibility and readability are inherent to successful communication. Although the terms are used interchangeably, differences between them do exist. Legibility refers to the recognition of individual letterforms and their relative position to other letters in word formation. The design of the typeface determines legibility. An illegible typeface will not be readable. Readability refers to how typography is presented to the viewer as words, lines, and paragraphs. It is influenced by the typographic arrangement, including line length, leading, and spacing. Readability is dependent on the designer and his or her ability to work with type effectively. If a text is unreadable, it is likely that it is poorly composed or the typeface is illegible; its application needs reconsideration or new typefaces should be chosen.

In certain applications, intentional illegibility for aesthetic—not communicative—reasons is desirable. For example, typographic information, such as letters, words, lines, and paragraphs, can be carefully crafted into layers, textures, or graphic forms that are intended for visual impact, not legibility or readability. The illegible letterform constructions become visual elements that add dimension and impact to the presentation of the design in combination with the primary textual content.

| *design* hat-trick design | A dominant photograph commands attention on the cover of this annual review. Subtle typography is composed simply along the bottom margin. It is diminutive yet easily distinguishable within the dark areas of the image by knocking out of the stock.

| *design* hat-trick design | Hand lettering adds distinction to the spacious interior spreads of this annual review. Even when not using traditional typefaces, it is important that all lettering maintain legibility and readability to convey the message of the design effectively.

objective and subjective representation

Although many methods of designing with type are used, they can be broken down into two forms of representation: objective and subjective. Objective representation is practical and straightforward. It is characterized by a clear, ordered presentation of information that is shared in a direct, efficient manner. The typographic arrangement systematically communicates, or denotes, its messages without relying on layers of textual content that imply additional meanings. The message is clear. Objective representation places no emotional impact on the viewer. Common examples include maps, charts, diagrams, and timetables.

Subjective representation is conceptual and interpretive. It is heavily focused on a theme or idea that creates an experience for the viewer. Allowing for greater complexity, subjective typographic solutions are often layered and textural, creating a blanket of language on the page. Connotative in nature, subjective representation provides multiple levels of interpretation for the implied meaning of the design. It appeals to the emotions of the viewer. Often poetic and expressive, many design projects can be subjective in nature, depending on their communicative function.

Whether a design is objective or subjective (or somewhere in between), the designer's task is to approach the text with a critical eye. Neither the kind of project or the amount of text dictates its typographic value. All text demands thoughtful and appropriate execution.

| **design** meghan eplett | *The typographic composition of* The Cat and the Fiddle *is musical. By using multiple type sizes and faces (Clarendon, Kabel, and Walbaum), the artist has made the text rhythmic. Letterforms effectively communicate the narrative through their dense textures that fill the spread and connote volume.*

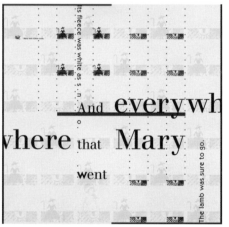

| **design** meghan eplett | *The viewer is led down and across the spread for* Mary Had a Little Lamb. *The type forms a path for the viewer to follow in the same way that the lamb follows Mary. The typography in* Jack and Jill *is composed along a dynamic angle. Its arrangement forces the viewer to read the text from the bottom right, up to the top-left corner, and down again. The unnatural direction encourages the viewer to make connections between the position of the type and its relation to the storyline.*

macro and micro perspectives A designer must approach the typographic layout with macro and micro perspectives. One deals with the overall design layout, whereas the other addresses its typographic intricacies. The macro view is concerned with the whole body of typography that makes up the design. Seeing all the content at once, the designer must establish the format of the composition as well as the typographic hierarchy and placement of elements.

Within the big picture, each individual element needs attention. By taking a micro perspective, the designer concentrates on the typographic details, such as kerning, spacing, and ragging, to ensure a clean presentation and consistent application. The attention to details refines the type and contributes to the success of the whole. Be sure to pay equal attention to both macro and micro perspectives—they are interdependent and equally important.

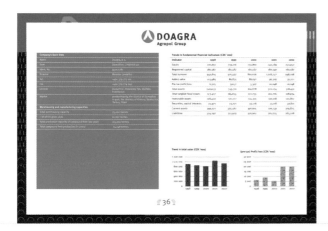

| *design* studio najbrt | *A page from this annual report features a number of tables and graphs, which are common examples of objective representation. Facts and figures lend themselves to clear, ordered presentations that deliver information simply and directly.*

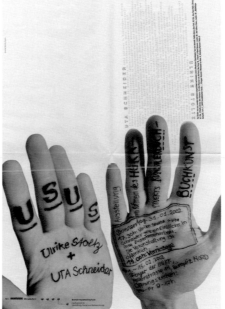

| *design* superbüro | *Alternative typographic treatments distinguish this set of posters. Unique letterforms draw attention and communicate with impact. Constructed out of plants and written on hands, the letters are conceptually appropriate; the plants symbolize Holland (home of Irma Boom), whereas the hands connote the left and right pages of a book (USUS are book designers).*

symmetry and asymmetry There are different ways to compose the typographic page: symmetrically or asymmetrically. Symmetrical compositions offer balance and harmony. They possess inherent stability that is approachable and understandable. However, symmetry can also be static and can lead to passive, lifeless typography that falls to the background. It can also be difficult to work with multiple typographic elements because there are too many factors to achieve balance. Regardless, the designer must find ways to create variety and visual emphasis within the symmetrical structure to keep the design interesting.

Asymmetrical compositions generate activity and motion—desired qualities in most applications. They support compositions with numerous typographic variables. Multiple alignment points provide unlimited options for the arrangement of the visual elements. Like symmetrical layouts, the designer still needs to achieve optical balance. The visual elements should not feel like they are falling down or tipping over. When working asymmetrically, use visual tension. Force typography to the edge of the page. Contrast large elements with small ones. Turn typography on its side, mixing orientations. Vary the depth of columns. Use graphic shapes and imagery to offset typographic elements. The possibilities are limitless.

| ***design* nb: studio** | A traditional, symmetrical composition demonstrates balance through the use of a single typographic column and contrasting black-and-white pages. Changes in type size provide variety within the text, whereas the unusual structure of the book promotes interaction.

| ***design* lichtwitz** | An underlying structure provides vertical alignment points for the placement of flush left columns of text, which feature the use of type weight to distinguish information. The left margin defines the active space of the page as well as the leading edge for dominant typography, which offsets the symmetrical arrangement of the six columns.

alignment Alignment refers to the horizontal and vertical positioning of typography within the margins. The edges of the page can also serve as alignment points if the type is strong enough and will not be trimmed off during production. The designer must use alignment to create visual relationships between the elements of the design; it helps unify the composition. The precise alignment of typography across and down the page cultivates harmonious spatial relationships and consistency. Grids and systems of proportions are needed to provide divisions of space to achieve alignment, which includes centered, flush left and right, and justified options. However, typographic settings often need subtle adjustments outside of the grid to create proper optical alignments.

typographic color Typographic color refers to the density of typographic elements and their perceived gray value—the overall feeling of lightness and darkness on the page. Color is affected by the typeface, horizontal and vertical space, and amount of text on the page. Achieving an even sense of color is generally ideal but not always appropriate. Too much evenness is dull and can result in a gray, static design. Typographic contrast and depth of color creates an active, rich composition with dark and light values.

| **design** 344 design, llc | *This book spread is carefully structured and composed along horizontal, vertical, and diagonal alignment points that create optical connections between the visual elements, strengthening and unifying the design.*

| **design** kontour design | *The variable density of the justified text blocks demonstrates perceived gray values. Typographic color is affected by the diverse styles, weights, and widths of Cholla. The composition exhibits depth and texture in its tightly packed arrangement and works perfectly because the text is not intended to be read in any particular order.*

type size Type size is measured in points. Large and small shifts in type size can make a significant difference between clarity and confusion, elegance and clumsiness. Changes in type size are effective methods to create hierarchy and add contrast to the page. In addition, remember that typographic application relies heavily on optical settings. For example, typefaces that are the same point size generally do not match in visual size. Adjustments are needed to harmonize their appearance. In addition, it is sometimes helpful to develop a proportionate scale of type sizes that will foster relationships and provide a range of options for all variables throughout the design. Though not all design projects require such detailed consideration of type sizes, it is useful to do studies and develop a system based on the content before beginning to design.

case Uppercase and lowercase settings have individual characteristics that make them useful in typographic application. Lowercase letters are more readable than uppercase because of their variation and white space in and around each letter (counters), as well their ascenders and descenders, which ease word recognition. Lowercase is ideal for most typographic applications, especially continuous text, because it is easier to read. Uppercase emphasizes letter-to-letter recognition, which slows down the reading process, making it impractical for large amounts of text. However, uppercase settings are used in limited instances for emphasis and to denote hierarchical text, for example headings or subheadings.

text from
Mixing Messages: Graphic Design in Contemporary Culture
by Ellen Lupton
Princeton Architectural Press,
New York, 1996

| *design* capsule | *Changes in type size, as well as case, add contrast and impact. On the recto page, bold capitals are large and command attention as the dominant text. The justified setting spans the page in an appropriate line length. The attached tag also presents variations in typeface and size to establish hierarchy.*

kerning and tracking Letterspace refers to the spaces between letters, whereas word space is concerned with the spaces between words. Adjusting letterspace and word space improves legibility and finesses letter-to-letter and line-to-line relationships to achieve an optically even setting. With any adjustments, whether loose or tight, always be consistent.

Kerning, also known as letterspacing, is used to adjust the slight distances between letters to avoid character collisions and irregular and unwanted spaces. Kerning fosters a uniform typographic texture that allows the text to flow and read smoothly. It is critical when setting text in large type sizes, because the spacing irregularities are more apparent. Common character combinations, including *Ty*, *Va*, *Yi*, *11*, and *19*, always require attention.

Tracking is concerned with the overall spacing of words, lines, and paragraphs and can improve readability. It also affects typographic color; tightly spaced text appears heavier and darker on the page, whereas open text appears light and gray. However, as letters get closer, collisions occur. As they move further apart, they lose their identity as words. A general rule is to avoid tracking lowercase letters, especially (almost always) in paragraph settings. The text becomes less legible and readable as spacing increases. However, very slight amounts may improve readability, especially with bold and condensed typefaces. Uppercase settings always demand tracking with a careful eye to increase legibility and readability.

Typography is the basic grammar of graphic design, its common currency.

TYPOGRAPHY IS THE BASIC GRAMMAR OF GRAPHIC DESIGN, ITS COMMON CURRENCY.

The variation in the shapes of lowercase letters, particularly ascenders and descenders, allows them to be recognized easily; while uppercase letters, which are uniform in height and width, require additional spacing to enhance their recognition.

| **_design_ kearneyrocholl** | *Uppercase settings are used on this cover for Area magazine. Attention to spacing (tracking) is evident and imperative to improve readability when working with capitals. As pictured, adequate leading is also needed between lines of capitals to enable accessibility from line to line.*

Type
default spacing

Type
corrected spacing

TYPE
default spacing

TYPE
corrected spacing

Kerning and tracking letterforms to appear optically even is always needed, especially in larger type sizes and capital settings, which demand tracking to open overall space and improve readability. Individual spaces between letters are kerned to achieve an optical balance by slightly shifting letters to the right or left. Relying on default settings or mathematics is often ineffective.

line length Like most typographic factors, line length depends on type size, leading, and column width, as well as the amount of text that needs consideration. If the line length is too short, the number of words per line is limited. Short line lengths are also problematic if the type size is too large. If the line length is too long, the viewer's eyes travel a great distance to read one line of text, which is laborious, and they can easily lose position or have difficulty moving down to the next line. As a general standard for continuous text, forty-five to seventy-five characters per line is the ideal length. Without always relying on strict rules, the designer must consider every factor to determine the most comfortable measure.

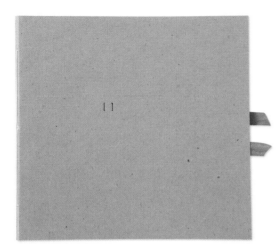

| *design* **renate gokl** | *The cover of the artists' book,* Seven Rules of Rikyu, *is minimally adorned with small brackets. The position is just outside the center of the page. Letterpress adds tactile, human qualities to design that computer-generated typography cannot achieve.*

| *design* **renate gokl** | *An interior spread is minimally composed in a spacious environment. Type size and position are used to achieve hierarchy among three texts woven into one spread (the harmonic offspring of ideal opposites and excerpts from* tea life, tea mind, *and* The Book of Tea).

Leading measures the space between lines of text and influences readability. Appropriate measures are determined based on typeface and size, line length, and x-height. In most cases, leading is greater than the type size used. For example, 10 point type over 18 point leading, which is marked 10/18. It can also be set solid, which means that the leading equals the type size, such as 10/10. If leading is less than the type size, it is called negative leading (10/8). When two pieces of text intersect between lines, it is called overlapping text. This technique can be used to integrate texts, while enhancing the typographic color and texture of the page.

leading Leading, the space between lines of text measured from one baseline to the next, greatly affects readability. If the design is made up of a number of typographic variables, it is critical to develop a system of leading intervals that will unite all the elements along a shared baseline. Typeface and size, x-height, and line length affect the need for more or less leading. For example, longer line lengths require more leading to accommodate the long horizontal motion of reading. Letterforms with tall x-heights, heavy and condensed type-faces, and sans serifs need more leading than shorter, lighter, wider, and serif typefaces.

In addition, if leading is too tight, it is easy to jump to the next line without finishing the first. If it is too loose, the text no longer appears continuous and could be read as individual lines instead of a series of connected thoughts. In most cases, the leading should be larger than the spaces between the words. Negative leading is leading that is decreased to a size less than the type size used, for example, 8 point type set on 6 point leading.

| **design** kinetic singapore |

The business cards are designed to allow each designer to express his or her voice by controlling the presentation of the message. By choosing the content, as well as its color (in the black column) and leading, the designer can personalize each card.

10/18

No matter how admirably we plan our work or how fine in design are the types we select, its appearance when printed depends on good composition—the combination of type into words, the arrangement of words in lines, and the assemblage of lines to make pages.

10/10 solid leading

No matter how admirably we plan our work or how fine in design are the types we select, its appearance when printed depends on good composition—the combination of type into words, the arrangement of words in lines, and the assemblage of lines to make pages.

10/8 negative leading

No matter how admirably we plan our work or how fine in design are the types we select, its appearance when printed depends on good composition—the combination of type into words, the arrangement of words in lines, and the assemblage of lines to make pages.

overlapping text

No matter how admirably
we plan our work or how
fine in design are the types
we select, its appearance
when printed depends on
good composition—the
Typographers on Type: An Illustrated Anthology
combination of type into
from William Morris to the Present Day
words, the arrangement
by Rauri McLean, editor
of words in lines, and the
W.W. Norton & Company, New York, 1995
assemblage of lines to
make pages.

paragraph settings Determining paragraph settings depends on the amount of text, type size, and line length. The designer must select appropriate measures that accommodate the text and fit comfortably within the shape of the page. These measures should enhance the format and activate the compositional space. Forcing the type to fit into unsuitable arrangements (paragraphs or other text) results in poor typography and discourages readability and viewer interaction.

There are four primary styles of paragraph settings: centered, flush left/ragged right (FL/RR), flush right/ragged left (FR/RL), and justified (FL&R). Centered text is positioned at an equal distance between two columns or margins. It is ragged along both sides. Centering is not ideal for longer texts because readability is hampered by the lack of a flush edge. Flush left text is evenly aligned along the left side, and the right side of the text is ragged. Used often, flush left text is highly readable. Flush right text is set solid along its right edge with a ragged left. Readability is lessened because the beginnings of each line are ragged. Justified paragraphs settings are flush along both right and left edges.

| **design** collaborated inc. |

This brochure features a series of headings and flush left paragraphs that move sequentially across the front of each panel. The layout functions in response to the accordion-fold format, which divides the composition into six sections. The shape of the page enhances the presentation.

centered

Determining paragraph settings depends on the amount of text, type size, and line length. The designer must select appropriate measures that accommodate the text and fit comfortably within the shape of the page. These measures should enhance the format and activate the compositional space. Forcing the type to fit into unsuitable arrangements (paragraphs or other text) results in poor typography and discourages readability and viewer interaction.

flush left, ragged right

Determining paragraph settings depends on the amount of text, type size, and line length. The designer must select appropriate measures that accommodate the text and fit comfortably within the shape of the page. These measures should enhance the format and activate the compositional space. Forcing the type to fit into unsuitable arrangements (paragraphs or other text) results in poor typography and discourages readability and viewer interaction.

| *design* blue river design |

The minimal design of the front
and back cover relies on subtle
typography to direct the eye into
the gallery booklet. The sparse
cover connotes the empty canvas,
preparing the viewer for the
range of artwork presented
on the interior.

| *design* blue river design |

Interior spreads can be viewed
horizontally and vertically. The
typography is clean and simple.
On the inside front cover, the narrow column mimics the shape of
the page. Another interior spread
pictures light, subordinate letterforms that support the imagery
in quiet, lowercase settings.

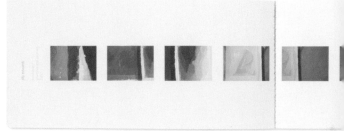

flush right, ragged left

Determining paragraph settings depends on the amount of
text, type size, and line length. The designer must select
appropriate measures that accommodate the text and fit
comfortably within the shape of the page. These measures
should enhance the format and activate the compositional
space. Forcing the type to fit into unsuitable arrangements
(paragraphs or other text) results in poor typography and
discourages readability and viewer interaction.

justified

Determining paragraph settings depends on the amount
of text, type size, and line length. The designer must select
appropriate measures that accommodate the text and fit
comfortably within the shape of the page. These measures
should enhance the format and activate the compositional
space. Forcing the type to fit into unsuitable arrangements
(paragraphs or other text) results in poor typography and
discourages readability and viewer interaction.

Paragraph settings include
centered; flush left, ragged right
(FL/RR); flush right, ragged left
(FR/RL); and justified (FL&R).
Centering connotes formality,
yet lacks the flush edges that
foster alignments with other
visual elements. Justification
is the most traditional setting
and features lines of equal
length. Flush left, ragged right
is commonly used because it
is easy to locate the beginnings
of each line, which enhances
readability. Flush right, ragged
left is a fresh alternative, yet
readability decreases because
the position of the beginning
of each line varies.

All paragraph settings, except justified, have fixed spacing, which means that the word spaces are consistent. Justified settings have variable spacing. The word spaces are flexible, depending on the number of words per line as well as the length of the line. Justified settings have variable spacing. The word spaces are flexible depending on the number of words per line, as well as the length of the line. Working with justified text is difficult. Without careful attention to type size and line length, visible holes, called rivers, often appear. Rivers are a series of inconsistent word spaces that create distracting open lines running vertically through the justified paragraph. Flush left and right and centered texts are generally easier and more flexible to work with and require fewer adjustments to achieve proper settings.

Beyond these settings, a paragraph can also be separated into individual lines of text that are composed without a consistent, flush-edge alignment from line to line. This is an ideal setting for smaller amounts of text that demand a looser, expressive composition. Layouts may feature the use of one or a combination of paragraph settings. However, take caution when mixing paragraph settings; creating inconsistent visual relationships could lead to disorder, and a scattered presentation of thoughts that can be difficult for the viewer to follow.

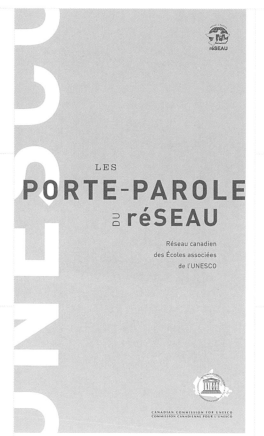

| *design* kolégram | The cover of Les Porte-Parole du réSeau *is composed in an optically centered, yet asymmetric, layout. The title treatment is composed as a solid unit that features well-spaced capitals and shifts in scale and orientation. The white letterforms to the left of the title break the color field and demonstrate how type can function as graphic form and provide impact.*

| *design* kolégram | *The first interior spread is composed with decisive hierarchy. A single justified column falls from the top margin. Its alignment, height, and width mirror the book format to create a harmonious relationship. A bold, uppercase title sits to the left of the body text with dominance, whereas a small page number rests on the bottom of the page.*

A good typographer is

one who can arrange type so as to produce

a graceful, orderly page that puts no strain on the eye.

This is the first and last

fundamental requisite of book design,

and like most operations,

it is a matter of years of training.

text from
The Form of the Book:
Essays on the Morality of Good Design
by Jan Tschichold
Hartley & Marks,
Washington DC, 1991

A paragraph can also be composed in an asymmetric configuration, which adds visual interest to the arrangement of the text. Although not appropriate for all applications (or extensive amounts of text), this setting offers flexibility and typographic invention.

REPRÉSENTANT LE QUÉBEC

Quand, à 18 ans, on est reconnu régionalement et qu'à 38 ans, on l'est internationalement, le cheminement semble tout naturel et pourtant ... Que de travail !

JOSEPH-RICHARD **VEILLEUX**

QUÉBEC

Joseph-Richard Veilleux possède depuis longtemps un bagage impressionnant de connaissances acquises à l'Université Laval reliées au monde des arts visuels, en histoire de l'art, en peinture et en couleurs avec des membres de l'atelier graphique de Bruxelles et du Centre de psychologie expérimentale et comparée de l'Université de Louvain en Belgique. Il a été professeur de perception visuelle au Collège Algonquin d'Ottawa et est détenteur d'une maîtrise en psychologie expérimentale de l'Université Laval. En 1977, il participe à la première biennale des artistes du Québec au Centre Saiddye Bronfman à Montréal. Depuis, il a participé à plusieurs expositions au Québec, au Canada, aux États-Unis et en Europe, Joseph-Richard Veilleux est membre de l'Académie royale des arts du Canada. Il siège sur de nombreux comités et conseils d'administration, dont celui du Musée des Beaux-Arts du Canada, à l'invitation de l'honorable Sheila Copps, ministre du Patrimoine canadien.

Né en 1948 à Saint-Georges, au Québec, Joseph-Richard Veilleux peut se vanter d'avoir fait suer bien des chroniqueurs. Son personnage et son œuvre insaisissables sont proportionnels à sa notoriété nationale et internationale. Un gars profond, un peu religieux, intérieur. Son travail pictural sur papier, toile, bois ou granite, en deux ou trois dimensions, célèbre l'imaginaire et la symbolique de l'existence. Travaillant à grands aplats, mêlant surfaces silencieuses et griffures bavardes, couleurs denses et tons évanescents, il démontre avec éloquence l'impasse de l'être. « Je ne veux rien saisir, je veux un art qui se tient, qui flotte, qui ascensionne, qui dérive entre le désir qui subitement anime ma main, et la politesse, qui est le congé discret donné à toute vie de capture ».

38_39

| *design* kolégram | *Interior spreads feature the same text: the name of a person or group, their country, one callout, body copy, and imagery. To maintain order, a consistent layout is applied. The last name (or group) is the focal point running up from the bottom of the page. It identifies each spread while giving it an individual spirit that breaks the monotony of the pages. The name also provides an edge for the callout text and country name, which sit in alignment.*

indents Indents are used to signal a change from the paragraph preceding it. (The first paragraph of any text does not require an indent because there is nothing that comes before it.) Indents vary in depth, depending on the type size and line length. Traditionally, indents are the size of an em, which is a measure of horizontal distance that is equal to the type size used. For example, if 8 point type is used, the em measure is 8 points. However, many alternatives are available. For example, add an extra line space between paragraphs. Even without an indent, the empty space is a visual cue indicating a new paragraph. Instead of adding space, insert typographic devices at the beginning of the paragraph, such as bullets, ornaments, or symbols. Hanging indents, also known as outdenting, features the first line set outside of the other lines that are indented below it. It is a good idea for the designer to experiment with indents so that he or she gets a sense of what functions appropriately with different designs.

spacing With the paragraph positioned in relation to the shape of the page, as well as the other typographic variables and visual elements, it is necessary to hone its finer details. For example, consideration of overall spacing is important; all type must be kerned and tracked as needed. For multipage layouts, be aware of the sequential flow of the text. Do not leave a short line with one or two words, or a widow, at the end of the paragraph, because it leaves too much white space on the last line and attracts attention as the only isolated element of the paragraph. Also, do not begin a spread with the last line from the previous spread. Likewise, do not end a spread with the first line of a paragraph that runs onto the next page. Both of these situations are known as orphans.

Hyphenation and ragging also require careful attention. Some simple suggestions to improve the appearance of text include avoiding more than two hyphenated lines in a row. Be alert to how words split. If possible, try to break them into even halves instead of leaving a stump at the end or beginning of a line. Never hyphenate proper names.

It is also important to adjust ragged edges of a paragraph. Manual line breaks for all paragraph settings will clean irregular edges. In some cases, inconspicuous adjustments in column widths, spacing, and type size are also helpful. Generally, take care to avoid angles, curves, holes, and shapes. Anything that diverts attention from readability needs to be remedied. The eye should not be led to empty spaces, truncated words, short lines, or ledges that extend too far beyond the average line length. Rags should appear even but not so even that they look justified. The designer must achieve smooth ebb and flow through the paragraph without distraction.

| *design* aufuldish & warinner |
The Robert Colescott & Glenn Ligon *catalogue features a combination of serif, sans serif, and display typefaces. The composition of visual elements is traditional, whereas the typographic treatment elicits a contemporary tone.*

ROBERT COLESCOTT & GLENN LIGON

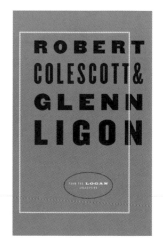

ROBERT COLESCOTT & GLENN LIGON

FROM THE LOGAN COLLECTION

hyphens, en dashes, and em dashes

The hyphen (-) is used for hyphenated words and breaking words in paragraph settings. The en dash (–) is used in compound terms and to separate items, for example dates, locations, times, and phone numbers. Although extra space is not needed before and after the en dash, the designer must carefully kern the spaces to avoid unintentional collisions. The em dash (—) is used to separate thoughts. There are no spaces needed before and after, but kerning may be required. Although the em dash is a more traditional method, the en dash can also be used to separate thoughts within a text because depending on the typeface, the em dash can appear too lengthy. When an en dash is used in this manner, spaces are added before and after the dash. If spaces are not added, the en dash closely resembles a hyphen and its function is lost. Whatever approach is chosen, use dashes appropriately and consistently based on their function within the design and according to the house style preferred by your clients.

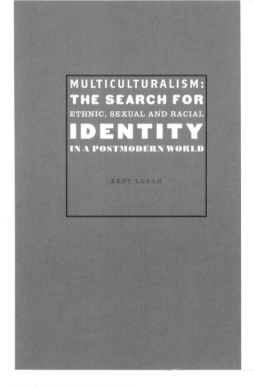

IT IS OFTEN SAID that "socio-political art" becomes dated very quickly and disappears from virtually all curatorial agendas. And while art that references overt, specific events or persons typically does not stand the test of time or memory, there have been several universal socio-political themes which have been a part of the fabric of society for the past thirty years and thus have transcended the narrow label of "socio-political art." In fact, art that is "relevant" to social issues is at the heart of the definition of postmodernism, and is often referenced under the umbrella of "multiculturalism."

As discussed above, Pop Art was a mirror on the popular culture of materialism and "keeping-up-with-the-Joneses" so prevalent in the 1960's. But as the decade drew to a close, darker issues clouded the horizon. The optimism of the early 1960's seemed to evaporate with the continued escalation of the Vietnam War and the concurrent growing antiwar sentiment at home; simultaneously, the Civil Rights Movement was in full swing, heightened by the assassinations of Martin Luther King, Jr., and Robert Kennedy in 1968.

Up to this point, mainstream artists only addressed socio-political issues obliquely. The first artist of stature who dared to do it directly was, ironically, the Abstract Expressionist painter, turned realist, Philip Guston. In 1970, Guston shocked the art world with his show of hooded Ku Klux Klansmen at the Marlborough Gallery. The evil images of Klansmen smoking, drinking, sitting around in empty rooms or patrolling streets reflected Guston's deep disenchantment with the Vietnam War, the oppression of minorities' civil rights and general political corruption and ineptitude. Leon Golub explored this same territory in a more graphic figurative manner. His paintings of torturers, mercenaries and thugs exposed the dehumanizing aspects of tyranny, abuse of power, oppression and the exploitation of the innocent. In a similar manner, the German artists Georg Baselitz and Anselm Kiefer held up a mirror to Germany's role in World War II and the Holocaust. Kiefer was often referred to as the "archaeologist of German guilt" and "as a kind of Pied Piper leading away from the demons of the Third Reich" (Bernard Marcade, *Flash Art*, Oct.-Nov. 1985). Baselitz's 1965 "hero" paintings of partisans and peasants rising out of the ashes of post-war Germany represented the hope that German society could rebuild and regain a sense of respectability and pride. In Britain, Gilbert & George's series of "photo-sculptures" referenced issues as far ranging as homosexuality, social stratification, racism, totalitarianism and the disillusionment of youth—all questions raging through British society at the time. In many ways these "legitimized" socio-political art for the artists of the 1980's and 1990's. In that regard, similar issues would be pursued by artists as diverse as Cady Noland, Ida Applebroog, Jean-Michel Basquiat, Jerry Kearns, Tom Otterness and the South African William Kentridge, as well as the whole first generation of contemporary Chinese artists.

Racism, segregation and black voter disenfranchisement had also reached a boiling point in the early 1970's. The artist who first embraced those issues was the "new image" painter Robert Colescott. His cartoonish, raucous images of blacks in distorted historical situations were a biting commentary on popular racial stereotypes. And despite progress in addressing the many aspects of African-American status within our overall society, this sub-

[67]

| *design* aufuldish & warinner |

Old style numerals, spaciously set capitals, and italic type run down the contents page in a centered alignment. Fitting into the central axis, two essay titles exhibit distinct changes in typeface, which include Clarendon, Bodoni, Champion, Brothers, Latin MT, and Gothic Round. The visual differences are diverse, yet harmoniously, composed. The density of the darkest letterforms contrasts with the lighter characters.

| *design* aufuldish & warinner |

A sample spread presents a justified paragraph setting for the treatment of the continuous text. Skillfully set in Bulmer MT, the text is the ideal size and line length for justification. The paragraph exhibits even spacing, ample leading, and hanging punctuation.

5'5"

Apostrophes and quotations marks are often inappropriately replaced with prime marks, which are used to denote feet and inches. Depending on the typeface, apostrophes and quotations marks, also known as smart quotes, are angled or curved and open or closed, whereas prime marks are straight up and down.

apostrophes, quotation marks, and primes

The correct use of apostrophes and quotation marks is a marked sign of the professional designer. True apostrophes and quotation marks are curved (' " ' ") or angled (' " ' "), depending on the typeface. They are also open (" ') or closed (' " ') to signal beginnings or endings. Apostrophes and quotation marks are not straight up and down (' "). These forms are prime marks, and they denote feet and inches. They should never be used in place of apostrophes and quotation marks.

| *design* nb: studio | *Interior spreads feature sans serif typography that is legible in its compositional simplicity. Hanging quotes are present along the flush left edge of the text. The hung quotes maintain the straight edge of the text and avoid unsightly indents to achieve optical alignment.*

hanging punctuation Optical alignment is a critical factor when designing with type. Anything that distracts the eye from reading needs subtle adjustments. This requires making minor adjustments to the text so it will appear aligned. For example, when punctuation, such as apostrophes and quotation marks, falls along flush edges of text, a slight indent is created that is visual distracting; the marks need tending to ensure that the letterforms optically align. Punctuation marks moved outside of flush edges maintain optimal visual alignment of the text. Demonstrating a high level of typographic refinement, hanging punctuation is a detailed process. However, page layout applications often provide features that easily support this action. Hanging punctuation applies to asterisks, apostrophes, commas, en dashes, hyphens, periods, and quotation marks. Other forms of punctuation that are the same visual weight as the letterforms, including parentheses, question marks, and exclamation points, do not need consideration.

FINAL THOUGHTS Designing with type can be tedious and time consuming but ultimately rewarding. Education, practice, and experimentation allow the designer to make intelligent, thoughtful decisions about typographic selection, application, and refinement while achieving a high level of visual intrigue and sophistication. Although there are many rules when designing with type, there is also a tremendous amount of flexibility to break them capably. Typography expressed with aesthetic grace is essential to clear communication and adds a level of sophistication to any design.

| **design** nb: studio | *Typography is used as texture and shapes the letters RSA that run across the front and back cover of the Royal Society of Arts brochure. An interesting graphic, the typographic texture is also functional—it is a running list of the 22,000 fellows of the organization.*

"There are two sides to typography. First, it does a practical job of work; and, second, it is concerned with artistic form."

default setting

"There are two sides to typography. First, it does a practical job of work; and, second, it is concerned with artistic form."

corrected setting

Working with typography demands attention to details, which includes hanging punctuation. To maintain the appearance of a flush edge of text, punctuation marks, including apostrophes and quotation marks, are positioned outside of the text.

text from
Typography: A Manual of Design
by Emil Ruder
Hastings House Publishers, Inc., New York, 1967

DESIGN

Form follows function—
that has been misunderstood.
Form and function should be one,
joined in a spiritual union.

FRANK LLOYD WRIGHT
architect

ANALYSIS

SEEING THE WHOLE AND ITS PARTS

The design process is evolutionary. It develops slowly and shapes the final design. The designer is actively involved with every aspect of the design process, from research and information-gathering to brainstorming and conceptualization, as well as experimentation, development, and execution. When the design nears completion at the end of the execution stage, the designer must analyze the design to determine its success or failure, asking several important questions:

Is the design engaging and informative?
Is the delivery of the message appropriate and clear?
Does the design reflect its function and purpose?
Are the visual elements cohesive?
Is there a logical progression through the design?

the importance of analysis

Analysis is the final stage of the design process. Thoughtful attention to, and evaluation of, the design ensures that all visual elements fit together like pieces of a puzzle. If one piece is out of place, the design is unresolved and the puzzle incomplete. The missing piece could be found through careful examination. It helps to begin the analysis by seeing the design as a transparent medium. Look through the piece and see all its layers to identify if the visual elements are orchestrated harmoniously. The designer must evaluate the design considering numerous factors, including appropriateness, communication, effectiveness, and integration. Other critical assessment criteria are hierarchy, legibility, movement, organization, sequence, and structure. In addition, the designer needs to examine color, composition, contrast, and form, as well as image, scale, space, and typography.

The design can be analyzed further by carefully checking the interdependence of the parts to the whole. The whole is the culmination, or final product, of the design process. It creates initial impressions, encourages interaction, and establishes the pathway that leads the viewer toward understanding. The parts are the essential factors (the team players) that solidify the design. Inextricably linked to every visual element, the parts enable and support the communicative function of the design; they cannot exist independently of the whole. No matter how dominant or subordinate, all the visual elements are meaningful. However, they exist successfully only in their symbiotic relationship to everything else.

| design nielinger & rohsiepe |

A visual system of color, image, structure, and typography is introduced on this calendar cover. The layout initiates viewer interaction, commands interest, and establishes the mood of the design.

| design nielinger & rohsiepe |

Looking at three months of the calendar, it is evident that a visual system is flexibly applied. A distinct identity for each month exists, yet all promote the unified essence of the design. Consistency is inherent, and the designer exploits the visual system through variation to keep it fresh.

| *design* 33rpm | Characterized by dramatic movement, the Pedro the Lion poster effectively demonstrates the use of scale to achieve contrast. The active, layered imagery falls from the top-right corner toward the askew title treatment and creates a logical, readable sequence that leads the viewer to the remaining pertinent information.

Působíme nejen v Praze, ale i v dalších 35 městech po celé republice a také na Slovensku.

www.caledonianschool.cz   ❖ Caledonian School   Corporate Language Training
Presentation 1

| *design* studio najbrt | Featuring a blue color palette, the Corporate Language Training Presentation 1 brochure uses color as an identifier to separate it from the other brochures in the series. The brochure also features repetitive square patterns and typography that are uniformly applied to maintain consistency, which is critical to the unity and success of the series.

| *design* studio najbrt |

An integrated series of brochures for the Caledonian School is consolidated into a harmonious package. Each of the four brochures is distinguished by its content and photography, as well as a unique color palette seen along the spines of each brochure to increase its accessibility.

evaluation considerations

Analysis checkpoints are needed throughout the design process to keep the project on track. They ensure that the designer considers everything and does not jump to the final solution too quickly. The designer wants to avoid any surprises at the end of the process that would demand a complete overhaul of the design. At the end of the execution stage, the designer should expect to thoroughly analyze the design in preparation for its final production—this is the primary focus of the design analysis stage. The designer examines not only the big picture but also the function and success of its parts.

When the design reaches the analysis stage, the designer is intimately familiar with it and must examine the layout with a fine eye and calculated hand. It can be a difficult task to step away from the design and evaluate it objectively. It is critical to remember that the design is intended for a specific viewer. The designer must be objective and remove any personal preferences from the analysis for the benefit of the design. When analyzing a piece, it is sometimes helpful to ask colleagues, as well as targeted viewers, to assist in the process because outsiders can provide fresh perspectives and easily assess the success (or failure) of the design.

| *design* **hendersonbromsteadartco.** |
The use of color, texture, and pattern, in addition to the carefully crafted letterforms, makes this poster engaging and distinctive. Its immediate impression effectively commands attention and leads the viewer into the piece for closer examination.

| *design* **hat-trick design** | *A clean, elegant letterhead demonstrates a successful balance between the communicative and aesthetic function of the design. Subtly accented with three lines of clear, readable typography, the spacious page allows plenty of room for correspondence with natural photography providing a soft background.*

THE **FUNCTION** AND **PURPOSE** OF ALL DESIGN PROJECTS VARY AND DEMAND DIFFERENT VISUAL APPROACHES.

A series of questions, which can be tailored to address individual projects, provides a starting point to begin the analysis of the design.

communicative function and purpose

Does the design reflect its function and purpose?

Is the delivery of the message appropriate, effective, and clear?

Does the design meet the client's objectives/goals?

Is there a balance between the design's communicative and aesthetic functions?

Is the design engaging, distinctive, and informative?

Does the integration of the visual elements create movement and rhythm?

Are the visual elements cohesive?

Does the design evoke the desired emotion, mood, and tone?

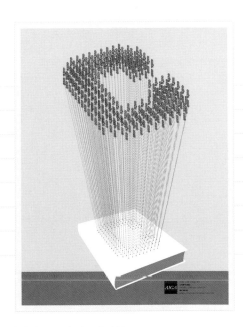

| **design** 344 design, llc | *The poster for the American Institute of Graphic Arts features book designer Chip Kidd and appropriately and effectively delivers the message by connoting his design work. The graphic illustration of the book is iconic, whereas its explosive cover exalts Kidd.*

basic compositional factors

Is contrast used effectively to distinguish all visual elements?

Does the use of space direct the eye toward the positive areas of the design?

Are changes in scale of the visual elements effective?

Is the quantity of information in the composition too excessive or minimal?

Does the design exhibit depth, dimension, and perspective?

Are orientation and position of the visual elements used advantageously?

Is tension between the visual elements effective?

Is repetition used appropriately and without adding too many visual elements to the page?

Does the use of color add value without overpowering or distracting the viewer?

Do the graphic shapes and linear elements enhance the design?

Do the illustrations or photographs connote appropriate emotions and meaning?

| *design* nb: studio | *The Knoll posters feature clever illustrations that create initial impact and communicate the individual characteristics of the furniture. Their dominant scale visually contrasts the subordinate typography, which quietly rests along the top and bottom margins. The use of color adds a strong background without overpowering the illustrations.*

structure and organization

for in-depth structure and organization information, refer to *chapter 5: structure+organization* building foundations

Is an underlying structure or method of organization evident?

Do horizontal and vertical spatial divisions provide alignment points for the visual elements?

Do the margins activate the positive areas of the design rather than frame the page?

Do the number of spatial intervals, columns, or modules suit the quantity of information?

Is symmetry or asymmetry used advantageously?

Are the visual elements consistently aligned across and down the page?

hierarchy

for in-depth hierarchy information, refer to *chapter 6: the interaction of visual elements* establishing hierarchy

Is there a logical progression (sequence) through the design?

Is a strong systematic hierarchy evident?

Are the visual elements ranked and visually organized into dominant and subdominant levels?

Does a dominant focal point lead the viewer into the design?

Does the ordering system provide accessibility, continuity, integration, navigation, and variety?

Is there evidence of foreground, middle ground, and background?

Does the design avoid monotonous or overactive visual fields?

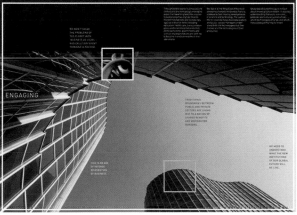

| *design* wilsonharvey/loewy |

The brochure spreads demonstrate an evident structure defined by three primary spatial intervals containing body text, which consistently falls from the top margin. The divisions of space also provide alignment points for additional visual elements, including photography and secondary typographic content.

typography for in-depth typographic information, refer to *chapter 7: typography* shaping the page

Does the typographic system encourage readability and comprehension?

Does the typography aesthetically invigorate the text with meaning?

If using multiple typefaces, is the combination harmonious and optically matched?

Are the typefaces sending the appropriate attitude and personality?

Are true italic and bold fonts used, not computer-generated italic and bold styles?

Do the paragraph settings enhance the shape of the page?

Are changes in styles, weights, and widths distinguishing content effectively?

Is typographic contrast and color evident?

Are ligatures applied, if available to the selected typefaces?

Are the typefaces legible and all text settings readable?

Are small capitals, as well as lining and non-lining numerals, used consistently?

Are all type sizes appropriate and not too small or large?

Are line lengths set in comfortable measures?

Is the leading between lines too tight or loose?

Does the typography need spacing (kerning and tracking) adjustments?

Do the paragraph settings suitably accommodate all the text?

Are all widows and orphans corrected?

Is attention paid to hyphenation and ragging?

Are indents used and consistently applied?

Are apostrophes and quotation marks used instead of prime marks?

Is attention paid to hanging punctuation?

Are hyphens, as well as en and em dashes, used correctly?

| *design* aufuldish & warinner |

A bold typographic treatment commands the masthead of the architecture journal arcCA. Changes in case, color, and scale create contrast in the masthead, as well as the subordinate text, to effectively distinguish content.

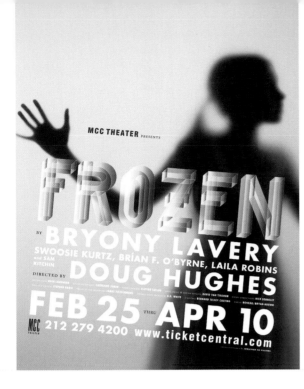

| **design** helicopter | *In the title treatment of the MCC Theater* Frozen *poster, letterforms are manipulated to create dimension. The stylized setting is contrasted by a sans serif typeface set in a range of sizes to achieve hierarchy. The uppercase settings are appropriately tracked with adequate leading to improve overall readability.*

FINAL THOUGHTS The design should be analyzed as a collective body of work that must function as a whole rather than as an assortment of unrelated parts. Without careful assessment of all the visual elements, the design may lack structure and organization, hierarchy, typographic proficiency, and, most important, value and meaning. The designer must pay close attention to every aspect of the design process and make careful and thoughtful decisions along the way. Always reinforce the message of the design through visual form that is consistently applied with decisive reason and aesthetic skill.

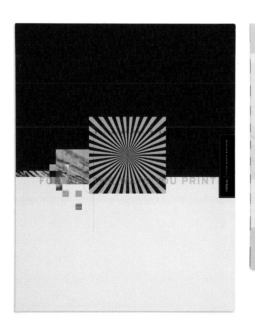

| **design** roycroft design |
The integration of the visual elements effectively unifies the cover and interior spread of this brochure. Photography, graphic shapes, linear elements, and typography are combined in a range of sizes to create movement through the design. Each element directs the eye toward another to maintain a rhythmic sequence.

Design is a plan for arranging elements
in such a way as best
to accomplish a particular purpose.

CHARLES EAMES
architect, designer

PROFILES

LOOKING CLOSER

AUFULDISH & WARINNER

When the California College of the Arts added the Masters of Architecture (mARCH) degree to their program, Aufuldish & Warinner was approached to design the materials announcing its inception. The first piece in the series was a poster introducing the new program and establishing the visual language system that was applied to later designs. At the outset of the collaboration, art director/designer Bob Aufuldish consulted with the client to discuss the project objectives. "What I started with was what not to do," says Aufuldish. "The client pointed to a wall of posters for architecture programs and lecture series and said that they all looked the same to him. And they did—they all used a very narrow design vocabulary." It was critical to establish an initial design that would contrast existing architecture programs yet still reflect architecture, as well as the California College of the Arts, in a fresh, unexpected manner.

After meeting with the client, the design process moved into the visual realm. "The idea of using jellyfish came to me quickly. Jellyfish ended up being perfect on numerous levels—visually, they are beautiful and perfectly suited to their environment; conceptually they make a clear connection to the idea of architecture as experimental structure. As a bonus, they speak to the college's location on the West Coast," explains Aufuldish. "Pyrex glassware was used to suggest the more rational side of architecture. I also liked the glassware for its references to chemistry and alchemy. The jellyfish and Pyrex contrast with each other conceptually and formally but are both are translucent and liquid, which helps unify them. I especially like the inside of the brochure where a jellyfish hovers above a flask like a ghostly vapor." Aufuldish next composed a cohesive design that combined organic imagery with rectilinear shapes and typography. "I was trying to communicate unconventional structure without showing a building or a model and without layering together imagery," adds Aufuldish.

The two-color brochure adapts the visual system developed in the poster. The typeface, Faceplate, is set consistently; the headings feature proficiently spaced capitals. Graphic shapes play a strong role in the structure of the composition. Transparent blue bars run across the cover and into the interior. Adding impact, they also provide baselines for the headings, as well as alignment points for the body copy.

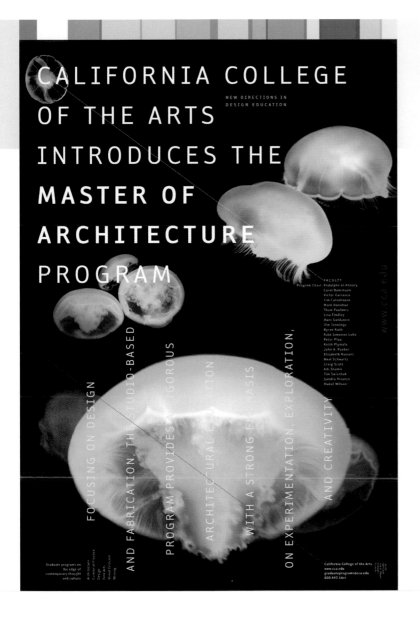

The California College of the Arts Master of Architecture poster takes an atypical approach toward the presentation of architecture. Using the jellyfish as a metaphor, the design features organic imagery combined with clean typography. Orientation, position, and scale establish hierarchy. Graphic shapes and linear elements provide subtle, structural reinforcement.

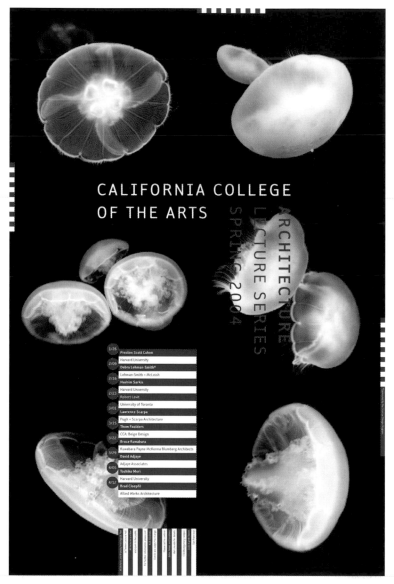

The fluid imagery glides on the surface of the brochure and posters, with graphic form adding color and providing the foundation for typography. Faceplate is the sole typeface; like the jellyfish, it is applied consistently and solidifies the visual system throughout all the pieces. Aufuldish further discusses the design: "The hierarchy is most complex on the master's poster because of the amount of text involved. Here, the hierarchy is controlled with color, size, position, and grouping. The brochure is a simpler matter because it's smaller and the majority of the text appears inside. The lecture series poster is structured simply— the design and placement of photographs is based on the way the poster folds."

The California College of the Arts, Master of Architecture brochure and poster, as well as the Architecture Lecture Series 2004 poster, are compelling designs that effectively communicate the client's message in an exciting, distinctive presentation. Using the metaphor of the jellyfish, as well the integration of color, form, and space, the pieces command attention. "The mARCH materials have been very successful," concludes Aufuldish. "The program completely filled its first class of thirty students."

*The California College of the Arts
Architecture Lecture Series 2004
poster combines imagery, graphic
shapes, and typography. Although the
jellyfish are distinctive, the system of
red and white rectangles adds visual
interest and defines the hierarchy.
Dominant information is placed within
the horizontal bars that appear inside
of the compositional space, along
the fold lines. Subordinate content
falls inside of the bars that align
on the outside edges.*

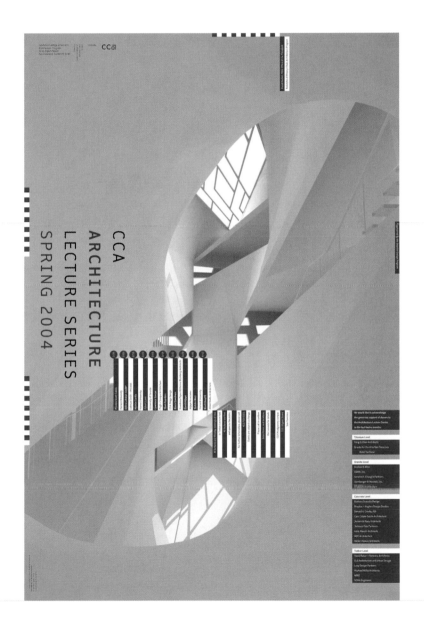

CAPSULE

designers brian adducci, greg brose, dan baggenstoss

Capsule presents a dynamic image in their letterhead system design, which includes envelopes, business cards, and mailing labels. "In designing our own stationery package, our goal was to develop a system that not only created a lasting impression but worked harder as a marketing tool than any brochure or website ever could," explains designer Greg Brose. Like all design projects, Capsule approached the project with a thorough methodology that included brainstorming, conceptualization, and exploration. "Once the name and philosophy was determined, we began by brainstorming metaphors that communicated explore, discover, and inspire," says Brose. (Explore, discover, and inspire are the primary themes of the identity system, as well as the philosophy of Capsule.) "Concepts were critiqued and refined until the final design and materials were chosen to reflect the personality of Capsule."

The design process involved the development of a visual language system that is applied throughout all the materials produced. The visual elements used consistently include the typographic treatment, color palette, vertical orientation of the Capsule logotype, and the condensed *C*, which is embossed on the letterhead and envelope and die cut on the business cards. Conceptually and aesthetically strong, the letterhead system also incorporates tactility and materiality into the design. "We wanted to use unique materials and textures to enhance the overall experience and engage the senses," adds Brose. Although textured paper is used, metal business cards demonstrate the most distinctive use of materials. Typography and linear elements are etched into both sides of the cards, and printed stickers allow for customization and the addition of color.

One of the significant elements of the Capsule letterhead system is its communicative value. Brose describes: "The design message comes to life in a way that creates a unique experience each time someone interacts with the stationery system. The recipient explores the artifacts and discovers the layers of meaning—a conversation is created around the meaning of the stationery system. For example, the golden section has been used as a fundamental design measure in art, architecture, and typography for centuries. In this context, we use it as a systematic element, which is sometimes confused with a ruler or decoration [on the business card]. Then, after a discussion around what the golden section measures—natural beauty—the participant learns something new. The result is an everyday example of our philosophy: explore, discover, and inspire."

The Capsule letterhead system engages the viewer and provides the opportunity to establish a design dialogue among designers and nondesigners. The design is sophisticated and presents a contemporary image. "The conversation that the card starts is a great way to warm up a meeting, presentation, or almost any discussion," comments Brose. Through unique materials and presentation, it has created a memorable experience for anyone we meet."

Etched business cards distinguish the system. They incorporate the consistent elements of the visual system, including the logotype and typographic treatment. However, they also communicate their philosophy—explore, discover, and inspire. Nicely spaced capitals interact on the back of the cards. Printed stickers add color to the metal forms, contrast the reflective surface, and call attention to the name of the designer.

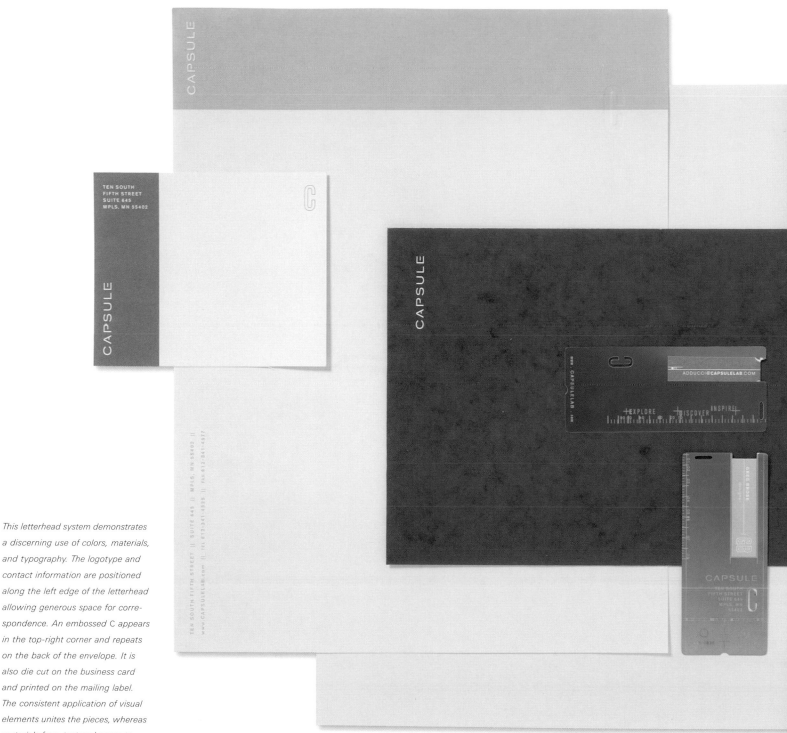

This letterhead system demonstrates a discerning use of colors, materials, and typography. The logotype and contact information are positioned along the left edge of the letterhead allowing generous space for correspondence. An embossed C appears in the top-right corner and repeats on the back of the envelope. It is also die cut on the business card and printed on the mailing label. The consistent application of visual elements unites the pieces, whereas materials from textured paper to metal provide contrast and tactility.

CHENG DESIGN

designer **karen cheng**

WORKING IN TWO-COLOR IS ALWAYS RESTRICTIVE,

BUT FRANKLY,

I WELCOME IT.

Seattle Arts & Lectures is a nonprofit literary organization "devoted to exploring ideas and imagination through language," describes designer Karen Cheng. They wanted to reinvent their "old-fashioned, even stodgy" image and produce collateral materials that would better reflect the variety of contemporary and prominent poets and writers participating with the organization. Seattle Arts & Lectures requested something "smart and fun," says Cheng, to complement their "intellectually challenging and interesting but not inaccessible or overly pedantic" events. The design was limited to two colors and inexpensive paper. Although these limitations may have excluded some possibilities, Cheng adds, "Working in two-color is always restrictive, but frankly, I welcome it. It helps narrow the design possibilities quickly."

The strength of the brochure series is the use of color and typography. Inspired by *The Interaction of Color* by Josef Albers, Cheng describes, "Each brochure is printed with only two colors. The colors are overprinted in a wide variety of screen combinations to create a four-color illusion." The brochure series adopts a modest yet rich color palette from bright yellow and warm orange to pale blue and deep green. Value and transparency are applied interchangeably throughout the series to distinguish typography, cast subtle light to photography, frame the page, and add graphic interest. The range of colors connotes value and sophistication from the brochure series while increasing their utility for Seattle Arts & Lectures.

teachers as scholars
2002-2003

2002-2003

nages: Telling the History of Modern Science /
and Metamorphoses / Crossing Borders, Crossing
, and Literature / Native Voices / How American
is Asian American Literature? / Shakespeare's Tragedies: Text, Interpretation, Production / America: A Sentimental
Adventure / The Great Migration / Latin American Artists and the Spanish Civil War

the Simpson Center for the Humanities and Seattle Arts & Lectures present

wednesday university

philosophy/ history/ literature/ culture

eamus Heaney
adie Smith
eorge Plimpton
rancine Prose
ndrea Barrett
avid Mamet

y Lecture Series 2002-2003

Seattle Arts & Lectures
15th anniversary season

four **poetry** readings
james tate | c.d. wright | louise glück | galway kinnell

presented by **Seattle Arts & Lectures** in collaboration with **ACT Theatre**
and **Open Books: A Poem Emporium**

*The systematic brochure series
for Seattle Arts & Lectures
dynamically takes advantage of
color, graphic shape, photography,
and typography. Designer Karen
Cheng sensitively exploits each
element and makes the most
of a limited budget to keep the
series diverse and unified.*

The typographic treatment for the brochure series is classically composed. The sans serif typeface—Interstate—is clean and modern. A variety of font styles, including italic and multiple weights, is exploited advantageously to shape a legible, ordered sequence through each brochure. The organization of the information relies on "typographic differences (size, placement, value, texture) to establish hierarchy," explains Cheng. In addition, the typographic treatment fosters consistency without monotony. Although the cover designs change for each brochure, the interior descriptive text is consistently applied throughout the designs.

The effectiveness of the brochure series is demonstrated by its reception from the client and viewers. "Seattle Arts & Lectures has had a very positive response to this 'rebranding' and standardization of their materials," says Cheng. "Many of their long-term subscribers have been specifically quite complimentary about the change in their materials." The final design, which is elegant in its pure, modern simplicity, is a reflection of the forces of the designer, client, and viewer coming together successfully.

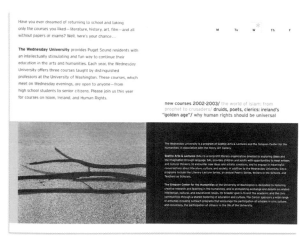

The composition of The Wednesday University *brochure is divided into halves. Photography and color draw the eye down and across the spread because of their visual weight and the horizontal design of the imagery, which flows seamlessly into a field of color.*

The Literary Lecture Series *brochure utilizes typographic size, position, and space to achieve an elegant, fluid hierarchy of the visual elements. The title sits boldly in the top-left corner of the composition. It draws immediate attention because of the emptiness that surrounds it; its isolation creates activity and prominence.*

Large, gentle photography draws attention to the Teachers as Scholars brochure (*left*). The photography is boldly contrasted by the dark field of color above it, which isolates a single quotation. The quotation, set in a small point size, rests quietly, yet with a strong voice, in the spacious rectangle. Type and image are complementary, providing visual impact and meaningful messages.

A colorful pattern of rules creates horizontal movement across the spread of the Four Poetry Readings brochure (*right*). The directional flow, which includes a string of photographs, draws attention to the typography that falls down the page in a cleanly composed, flush-left alignment.

COLLABORATED INC.

designer, illustrator, copywriter james evelock

The *Collaborated Mind* is an inventive promotional piece that functions on two levels: it is a brochure that sequentially unfolds into a double-sided poster. Designed by James Evelock of Collaborated Inc., the design engages the viewer because of its intelligent content and visual presentation. "As a promotional item, the piece needed to capture attention immediately. I wanted the company to appear as serious thinkers, yet cool," explains Evelock. Through the metaphorical use of the left and right brain, the design reveals insight into thought processes, as well as the design methodology of Collaborated Inc. The poster states, "Design is a whole brain process at Collaborated. We're using both sides of the mind to develop smart and original solutions to our clients' creative problems."

The *Collaborated Mind* promotional piece is diagrammatic in presentation. Visually reflecting the relationship between art and science, the piece is inspired by "a medical school human anatomy textbook I found on the street and annual report charts," notes Evelock. To hone the concept, "I began thinking about where art and commerce came from, and the idea of being right or left brain emerged. The idea seemed like a perfect fit for the company," states Evelock. "I really like the idea of pairing graphic design capabilities with a concept not regularly associated with graphic design—science." The design integrates charts, illustrations, and typography— all of which are kept to a minimum. "I felt if I explained too much about right and left brain activity, the readers would be turned off thinking it was a scientific direct-mail [piece]," comments Evelock.

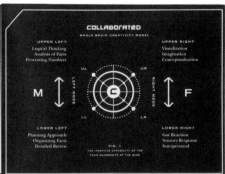

Opening the brochure on the side asking "Are you a righty?" leads the viewer through the multifunctional piece. The recto page contrasts the differences between the left and right brain. On the left side, a large arrow directs the viewer to the next fold, which opens to a long, narrow spread addressing female creative attributes. The presentation is cleanly composed. White text, illustrations, and graphic shapes are centered within the spacious, black field. Unfold again and find the male attributes, as well as the first glance at the poster.

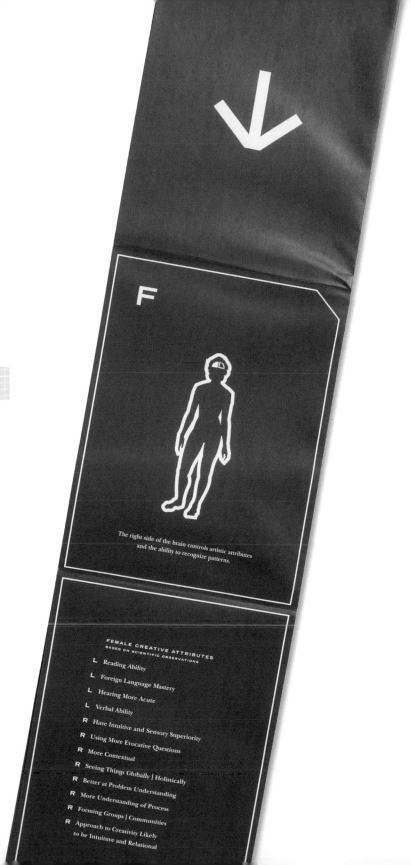

F

The right side of the brain controls artistic attributes
and the ability to recognize patterns.

FEMALE CREATIVE ATTRIBUTES
BASED ON SCIENTIFIC OBSERVATIONS

L   Reading Ability

L   Foreign Language Mastery

L   Hearing More Acute

L   Verbal Ability

R   Have Intuitive and Sensory Superiority

R   Using More Evocative Questions

R   More Contextual

R   Seeing Things Globally | Holistically

R   Better at Problem Understanding

R   More Understanding of Process

R   Forming Groups | Communities

R   Approach to Creativity Likely
    to be Intuitive and Relational

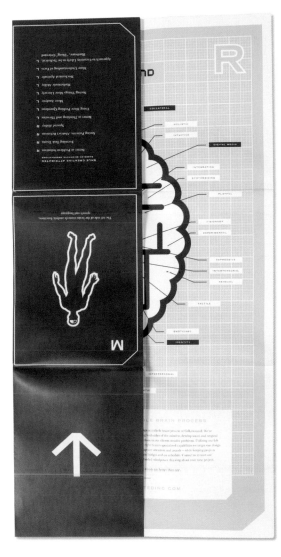

R

MALE CREATIVE ATTRIBUTES
BASED ON SCIENTIFIC OBSERVATIONS

R   Better at Problem Solving

R   Feeling Task Driven

R   Seeing Pattern, Abstract Relations

R   Spatial Ability

L   Using More Probing Questions

L   More Intuitive

L   Better at Thinking and Theories

L   Seeing Things More Linearly

L   Mechanical Ability

L   Mechanical Aptitude

L   More Understanding of Facts

    Approach to Creativity Likely to be Methodical,
    Illustrative, "Thing" Oriented

The left side of the brain controls analytic functions,
speech and language.

M

Large letters on a dense, black field provide an initial, mysterious impression and lead the viewer into the design. The folded piece presents the questions "Are you a righty?" or "Are you a lefty?" on opposing sides. From this point forward, the viewer makes a decision and moves through the design, learning about the left and right brain. When completely unfolded, a bright blue poster is revealed that further explains the function of the piece.

Both intriguing and informative, *The Collaborated Mind* brochure and poster is a refreshing approach for a promotional piece. It educates the viewer about the thoughtful considerations that go into the design process in a creative presentation. Commenting on the function of posters, Evelock adds, "I consider the poster to be one of the most important media within the graphic design field and felt it would be one of the most attention getting ways to communicate." The design supports this statement; it is visually strong and teaches the viewer about the science of the mind, as well as the science of graphic design. "I knew *The Collaborated Mind* poster would work from the moment I thought of it," concludes Evelock.

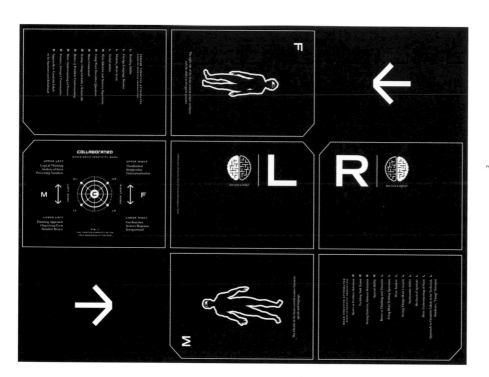

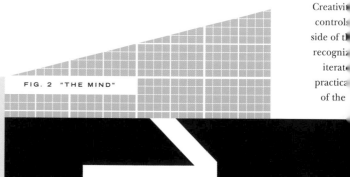

FIG. 2 "THE MIND"

Creativi
control
side of t
recogni
iterat
practica
of the

The Collaborated Mind *promotional piece is conceptually strong and visually engaging. Combining simple graphics and minimal text, the poster is highly readable, but scientific in feel. To counter the text, which discusses the function of the left and right brain, the layout of the poster is composed in the center of the page. The design simplifies the complex subject of left- and right-brain activity in an approachable and clever way.*

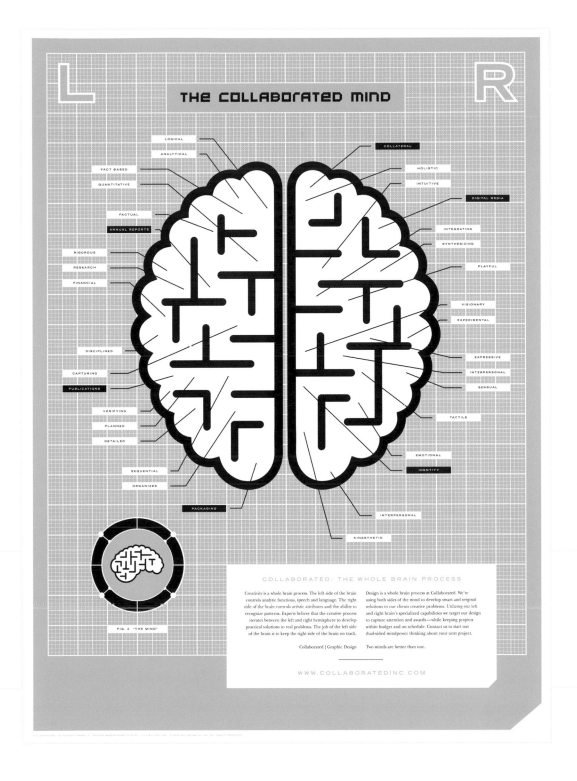

FIG. 2 "THE MIND"

COLLABORATED: THE WHOLE BRAIN PROCESS

Creativity is a whole brain process. The left side of the brain controls analytic functions, speech and language. The right side of the brain controls artistic attributes and the ability to recognize patterns. Experts believe that the creative process iterates between the left and right hemisphere to develop practical solutions to real problems. The job of the left side of the brain is to keep the right side of the brain on track.

Design is a whole brain process at Collaborated. We're using both sides of the mind to develop smart and original solutions to our clients creative problems. Utilizing our left and right brain's specialized capabilities we target our design to capture attention and awards—while keeping projects within budget and on schedule. Contact us to start our dual-sided mindpower thinking about your next project.

Collaborated | Graphic Design

Two minds are better than one.

WWW.COLLABORATEDINC.COM

Washington University in St. Louis,
School of Architecture, Graduate Programs Bulletin

designers jilly simons, regan todd
copywriter peter mackeith
photographers various

CONCRETE [THE OFFICE OF JILLY SIMONS]

Building on a five-year relationship, Concrete worked with the School of Architecture at Washington University in St. Louis to develop the *Graduate Programs Bulletin*. "Initially, I visited the school and had conversations with many of the faculty and students," explains designer Jilly Simons. "I spent a considerable amount of time working with our client developing concepts and exploring a variety of ways to introduce the idea of interactivity and 'making' into the piece."

The time spent in the research and information-gathering phases contributed to a concept "inspired by the school's identity, which resonates with the diverse realities of its multiple locations," states Simons. Reflecting internationality, the conceptual direction of the design, as well as its structure, is connected to the cover phrase, *Architecture in the world. Architecture in the making*. The bulletin captures the duality of the phrase by being divided into two sections. "The two-color 'hardworking' front matter covers the information about the school—its curriculum, faculty, and admissions," discusses Simons. "In contrast to the uncoated front section, we introduced five full-color gatefolds, on a coated sheet, at the back of the piece. This back section serves as a travelogue through different international studios and student work."

The design of the Graduate Programs Bulletin *is rich with details that solidify the design. On the cover, a thin white rule connotes the equator and divides the phrase,* Architecture in the world. Architecture in the making.*, which is the theme of the design. Circular die cuts fall above or below the horizontal center and reveal typography that notes the locations of the international program.*

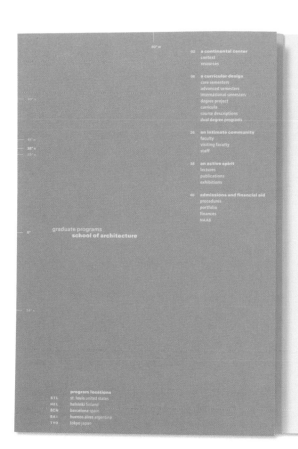

graduate programs
school of architecture

program locations
STL   st. louis united states
HEL   helsinki finland
BCN   barcelona spain
BAI   buenos aires argentina
TYO   tokyo japan

The School of Architecture at Washington University in St Louis cultivates the designer's identity as a leader: as both an expressive individual and a socially responsible citizen. The School's commitment to the ethical practice of architecture spans disciplines, contending cultural theories, and the range of representational media. The School's curriculum emphasizes the physicality of design through regard to site, purpose, material, technique and meaning. The School's identity resonates with the diverse realities of its multiple locations: St. Louis, situated at the virtual center of the United States, at the confluence of the Mississippi and Missouri river ecologies, possessing a rich architectural heritage and a complex urbanity; and international semesters in Barcelona, Spain, Buenos Aires, Argentina, Helsinki, Finland, and Tokyo, Japan—all cities of vibrant architectural cultures. The diversity of the Faculty, Visiting Faculty and the student community embodies this expansive intellectual territory. Intertwined with the School's character is the continuous thread of modernism's many-faceted, optimistic vision. This prospectus invites you to participate in the graduate programs of the School of Architecture at Washington University in St. Louis: **architecture in the making, architecture in the world.**

Interior spreads demonstrate the typographic system applied throughout the design. Quay Sans is the dominant typeface featured. It is combined with Univers to present a contemporary image. Their application features subtle changes in color, size, style, and weight to organize the content hierarchically.

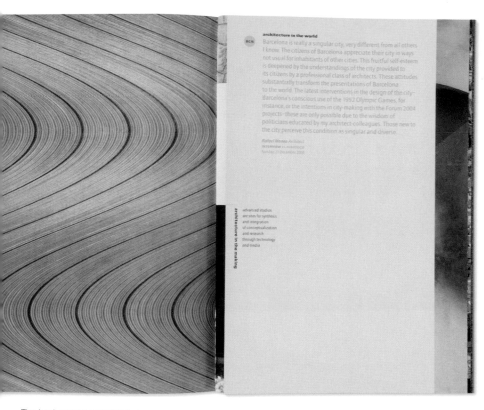

Both sections of the *Graduate Programs Bulletin* adhere to an effective system of organization. A consistent grid, color palette (blue and yellow), and typographic application are evident. Variation within the primarily typographic layout, including the use of color, size, style, and weight, establishes a clear hierarchy. The sudden appearance of color photography is the surprise element of the design. It is expansive and brings the viewer into new architectural environments, while evoking the global opportunities the program provides.

The *Graduate Programs Bulletin* is composed with conceptual strength and aesthetic agility. It presents an intelligent, professional image of the School of Architecture and incites the interest of potential students. "The client reported that the bulletin was extremely well received by faculty, students, and prospective students," concludes Simons. "Although the bulletin itself cannot claim full responsibility for the increase in enrollment inquiries, it can be attributed some of the success."

The back matter contains five gatefolds that highlight the international graduate studios. The recto page is purely typographic and contains insights from architects of the featured countries. The facing page is a dynamic, full-bleed photograph. When the gatefold is opened, the spread presents drawings and models. The final pages add intrigue and contrast with the objectivity of the front of the bulletin.

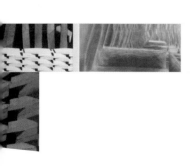

COOK DESIGN

art director/designer gary cook
editor marcus simmons

A conventional, staid GRID would have killed THE PICTURES.

Cook Design was approached by Racer Communications, Inc., to redesign *CART* magazine and "raise the profile of Champ Car racing, making it appear more glamorous, exciting, and closer to Formula One," explains art director/designer Gary Cook. The previous image of the magazine was a "very business-led look," adds Cook, which did not accurately portray the intensity of car racing. The client aspired to invigorate this ineffective impression with modernity and sophistication to entice potential advertisers to invest in the sport.

AND RACING

Just what is it that you have to do to make that pass in the   heat of a Champ Car race? We asked the stars...

CART *features expressive photography that activates its pages and glamorizes car racing. The viewer feels like they are a part of the action. The imagery connotes speed; the sensation also influences the typography, which appears to be in motion as it fluidly runs horizontally across the spread.*

To begin the design process, Cook Design experienced the racing scene firsthand during numerous photo shoots that defined and inspired the rest of the process. The objective of the design was to capture the "energy of the shoots," states Cook. He wanted the viewer to "feel like someone walking around the track with an 'access all areas' pass. I felt the design had to be very raw."

Vivid color and black-and-white photographs (shot by fashion and specialist car photographers) are the strength of the design and connote drama, energy, motion, and speed. The images are rough and smooth, beautiful and jarring. They capture the allure and attitude of car racing and add insight into the personalities of the drivers. Featuring sharp angles and perspective, the photography creates dimension and dynamism in each spread. In addition, the structure and organization of the design is dictated by the photographic imagery. The designer composes "a minisequence of pages based on the best pictures," describes Cook, "to end up with a run of pages that work in both a visual and informative sense."

The contents spread sets the standard of large-scale photography seen throughout the magazine. The imagery is complemented by straightforward, minimal typography set to the right side of the design.

Cook Design reinvented the image of CART magazine and created a visual environment that is edgy and vibrant. The cover introduces the aesthetic of the design. Vivid photography is complemented by clean typography, whereas scale and perspective are used to achieve drama, tension, and variety.

CART is typographically simple, which contrasts with the active photography and augments the character of the magazine. Gridnik, the dominant typeface used, has an industrial look that supports the objective of the design. Large numbers are applied as graphic shapes that create divisions of space on the page. The thin, oversized letterforms provide structural edges for the arrangement of body text. The photography and typography work together to shape a flexible grid dependent on the needs of each spread. "A conventional, staid grid would have killed the pictures," says Cook.

CART is energetic, fresh, and polished and infused with a refined design sensibility. "The client was very pleased, and the fans' message boards were alive for weeks when the magazine came out," adds Cook. "I think people were excited by how different it was—people found it very unexpected." According to Cook, the only downside of the design was "the fire ants that populate the Sebring circuit and how much it hurts when you lie on the floor to take a picture then realize they are biting your arm."

6 awesome challen- ges

Champ Car drivers face a range of mountains to conquer. In the coming pages, past champs Cristiano da Matta and Juan Pablo Montoya reveal six of the absolute toughest

words/ Tom Clarkson, Mark Hughes & Niki Takeda

DAZ- E OF DAYS

The very existence of a Champ Car driver seems

photography/ Peter Zownir

9:18

Interior spreads illuminate the personalities of the drivers, bringing their characters to life. The photography is dynamically composed to bring the viewer into the spatial environments. Large typographic elements, particularly the headings and large numbers, add a graphic texture and informative layer on top of the imagery.

Oval /sensations

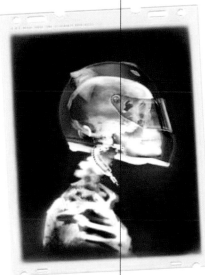

Relying on **blind faith**

ONE of the most famous sights in the world of Champ cars – negotiating bends almost without compromise in taking a bungee-jump blindfolded. It reached infamy as the place where Alex Zanardi went off course to snatch a last-gasp Champ Car victory from Bryan Herta in 1996. Juan Pablo Montoya talks us through it... "It is a fast corner to drive, and yes it is pretty dangerous, but I like it. Since Gonzalo Rodriguez got killed there it was scarier but still there is only one line really. You go over the crest, then all you see is a tree right in front of you, you basically point yourself at the tree. Then you suddenly drop, and then you are already on the curbs. I never had major moments there. I had bigger scares elsewhere than in the Corkscrew."

Juan Pablo Montoya, 1999 Champ Car champion; 2003 Formula 1 star.

ON an oval a driver can rarely transcend his car. Such are the high speeds generated on ovals that set-up is something of a black art. For this reason, Cristiano da Matta cannot single out an individual corner; but he reckons that if you get to Turn 4 on lap 250 of The 500 at Fontana, you'll be doing pretty fine... "From a driving point of view ovals are about minimum steering input. As a track, Fontana is one of the harder ones because you need to be able to run in three different grooves during the race: high, medium and low. If you can't, you will finish nowhere because the speeds are high and you will lose too much time overtaking people. What groove you can run in is all in the set-up and, sadly, a good high-groove car makes a bad low-groove car, and vice versa. It's a compromise, but one you have to maximize."

On a Champ Car superspeedway such as Fontana, the drivers regularly experience forces of more than 4G (four times their body weight). That's the point at which the US military requires its pilots to wear pressurized G-suits to ensure a regular supply of blood to the brain

24

CREATIVE INC.

creative director mel o'rourke
designer katie quinn

The Broadcasting Commission of Ireland is responsible for the activities of television and radio services, including developing standards for programming and advertising, as well as licensing independent broadcasting services. Creative Inc. was brought in to design the commission's annual review with the objective of communicating their broad range of services and many achievements throughout the year. The client also wanted the design to be visually unique and dynamic, as well as expressive of the progressive attitude of the company.

The visual approach toward the annual review was inspired by design styles of the 1950s, including "the way black-and-white photography was treated with a wash of color, as well as the graphic treatment of sound waves," explains creative director Mel O'Rourke. With an aesthetic direction established, Creative Inc. cultivated multiple visual ideas that would best represent the commission. The concept driving the piece was "to take key milestones and achievements from the year, represent these milestones through photography, and link them with large, graphic sound waves," adds O'Rourke. "This created a very visual introduction to the annual review, which needed few words to communicate the vast range of activities the [Broadcasting Commission of Ireland] were involved in."

A subdued cover, featuring large embossed numerals, is a quiet start to the active design that lies inside. The simple title treatment—set in Converse DIN—in addition to the Broadcasting Commission of Ireland logo, accents the top edge of the page. The elements define the margins and establish the consistent location of headings throughout the design.

In contrast to the cover, the contents page is bold and dynamic. Large, stable letterforms, set in Helvetica, clearly note each section of the annual review. The change in color between the text and numerals provides contrast, which enables easy identification.

Black-and-white photography fills the spread. The monotone imagery is also given a wash of color that provides a rich tone. The visual element dominates the page, whereas typography, set in a pale gray hue and composed just under the bottom edge of the image, takes a subordinate role.

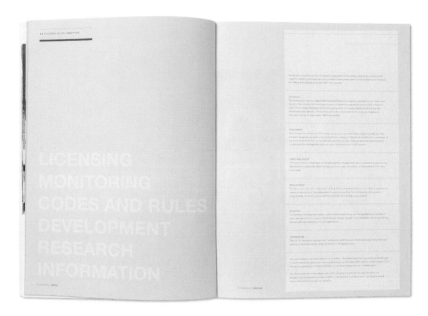

The oversized format of the annual review is commanding and presents a strong image of the company. In addition to the shape of the page, the soft and contemporary color palette is also distinctive. Large photography, graphic shapes, and fields of color provide depth within the compositional space. The scale of the visual elements is dramatic and adds variety throughout the design. A three-column grid divides the page into vertical divisions that accommodate the placement of the body copy, which is set in Converse DIN. Changes in type color and weight (from light to medium) create hierarchy within the primary text. In addition, large typographic elements, which are set in Helvetica, create a bold visual impression and clearly communicate messages. O'Rourke comments, "We knew the kind of image the [Broadcasting Commission of Ireland] wanted from their original brief, but it was our intuition that carried us through when making decisions regarding layout, colors, and style. We had a gut feeling for what would work."

The Broadcasting Commission of Ireland annual review "visually represented their achievements throughout the year in a clear, easy-to-understand fashion, whereas the fresh, modern style of the layout, typography, and photography conveyed their forward-thinking as an organization," concludes O'Rourke. "The piece was successful for us because it was a collaboration between us and the client. The client knew what they wanted and trusted us to deliver their message. These are the ingredients for the success of any project of this nature."

Additional interior spreads take advantage of the contemporary color palette. Full bleeds of the rich colors provide strong background fields for the placement of the textual content. In addition, the page is divided into three columns, which provides a flexible structure that accommodates body text and callouts in a range of type sizes.

Visible Language, *Issues 34.1 and 34.2*

KRISTIN CULLEN

designer kristin cullen
design consultant thomas ockerse
editor sharon poggenpohl

Issues 34.1 and 34.2 of the design journal *Visible Language* are a special series that focus on the subject matter, "words in space." The project was approached as an opportunity to explore the balance between practical and poetic design solutions. I was fortunate to be given a great deal of freedom, which allowed me to design the journals in a way that I felt best represented the content. The design also explores the role of typography as a voice that engages the viewer and leads him or her into the depths of the written word. It is visually complex and, at times, questions readability but does not lose it. The layout forces the viewer to interact with the design to glean its meaning. The journals are challenging and it does take time to navigate through each article—it's not intended to be an everyday experience.

To develop the concept, I considered the experience of reading and its relationship to typography. I wanted to activate the book space for the reader and illustrate how type can be presented as true to its meaning as possible. I value the idea that type is meant to rest silently on a page. There's an undeniable beauty to this approach. However, I was making a conscious effort to encourage the reader to interact with the typographic path laid out for them. I wanted the reader to not only see and read the words but feel like the words were talking to them.

The covers for Visible Language *work together to establish the mood of the journals. Projected letterforms are manipulated to create depth and perspective. The typographic environment is a reaction to the title of the series,* Words in Space.

Visible Language has been concerned with research and ideas that help define the unique role and properties of written language. A basic premise of the journal has been that writing/reading form an autonomous system of language expression on its own terms. To this must be added research and ideas that help define the presentation of information within the digital arena. The shift from page to screen is comparable in its significance to the shift from manuscript to print. Developing the knowledge base and conventions for this new media will take time and challenge our ability to move beyond the book and into more fluid, relational and responsive systems of presentation.

WEBSITE
www.id.iit.edu/visiblelanguage

POSTMASTER
send address changes to:
Visible Language
Rhode Island School of Design
Graphic Design Department
2 College Street
Providence, Rhode Island 02903

EDITOR AND PUBLISHER
Sharon Helmer Poggenpohl

DESIGN CONSULTANT
Thomas Ockerse

DESIGNER
Kristin Cullen

CIRCULATION MANAGER
Carrie Harris

FOUNDER
Merald Wrolstad

Cover Photography and Design
Kristin Cullen and Cheryl Hanba

GUEST EDITOR Sharon Helmer Poggenpohl

WORDS IN SPACE

ISSUE 34.2

PART ONE
Words in Space: An Introduction
Sharon Helmer Poggenpohl
The Restaurant at This End of the Universe:
Edible Typography in New Zealand
Sydney Shep
South of the Border
Maria Rogal
Word Space / Book Space / Poetic Space:
Experiments in Transformation
Lucinda Hitchcock
Reflections on Words in Space
Sharon Helmer Poggenpohl

Published continuously since 1967, Visible Language maintains its policy of having no formal editorial affiliation with any professional organization — this requires the continuing, active cooperation of key investigators and practitioners in all of the disciplines which impinge on the journal's mission as stated above.

©Copyright by Visible Language
Published tri-annually in January, May and October

VISIBLE LANGUAGE 34.2
Special Project of Visible Language in Two Issues

Deux ou Trois CHOSES Que Je Sais d'Elle

Partway through DEUX OU TROIS CHOSES QUE JE SAIS D'ELLE Juliette Janson (Marina Vlady) and her friend Marianne (Anny Duperey), both of whom belong to the world of high-rise housing complexes outside Paris and work as prostitutes to support their suburban lifestyle, visit a frequent client of Marianne's, an American newspaper reporter played by Raoul Lévy, one of the film's producers. As they enter his hotel room, Marianne carries a book with her. After undressing and seating herself on the bed to await him, she opens the book and reads silently. Marianne's act of reading emphasizes her nonchalant attitude toward being a prostitute. Waiting for her client, she reads as others might read while waiting for a bus or a train, as Bruno Forestier reads his copy of Maurice Limat's *l'Ecoute l'Univers* in LE PETIT SOLDAT (1960) to kill time during a railway journey. Like Bruno's, Marianne's book is the work of a prolific science fiction writer, for she reads *Un Remede à la Melancolie*, a translation of Ray Bradbury's collection of short stories, *A Medicine for Melancholy*. The book's title conveys the general idea that Marianne, Juliette and others like them who are caught with modern consumer culture desperately need a cure for their malaise. In addition, the presence of the book **emphasizes the gap**

between the imaginative world
Bradbury represents and the quotidian world of suburban Paris in the mid 1960s.

With the Bradbury volume, Godard also continues to use books as references to contemporary filmmakers, for the book obliquely alludes to François Truffaut. Earlier that same year Truffaut had released his Bradbury adaptation, FAHRENHEIT 451. Godard

had visited Truffaut at Pinewood Studios shortly before shooting began,[1] and Truffaut had paid tribute to Godard in the film with a reference to À BOUT DE SOUFFLE (Breathless, 1960). During the book-burning sequence at the house of the old woman who hoards books, Truffaut had included an image of *Cahiers du Cinéma* displaying a picture of Jean Seberg as Patricia Franchini on its cover. With the Bradbury reference, Godard returns the favor, though the implications of his friend may not be entirely flattering. Regardless of their artistic kinship, Godard was indebted to his friend in a more tangible way, for Truffaut, like Raoul Lévy, was one of the producers of DEUX OU TROIS CHOSES. Casting one producer as a prostitute's client and using her book to allude to another, Godard exposes her to both and therefore doubly reinforces an ongoing critique extending at least as far back as LE MÉPRIS (Contempt, 1963). Paralleling the prostitute's task with the film director's, Godard presents one of his "most deep-rooted theories":[2]

"to live in Parisian society today, at whatever level or on whatever plane, one is forced to prostitute oneself."[2]

The particular edition of the Bradbury work Marianne reads belongs to the science fiction series, Presence du Futur. The series title reinforces a persistent theme in Godard's work, the interrelationship of past, present and future. It also echoes an idea Godard articulates in his whispered voiceover during the memorable coffee cup sequence in DEUX OU TROIS CHOSES as he explains how the "lightning advances of science give to future centuries a haunting presence" and anticipates a time "when the future is more present than the present, when distant galaxies are at my door."

ADVISORY BOARD

COLIN BANKS
Banks and Miles, London
NAOMI BARON
The American University, Washington, D.C.
FERNAND BAUDIN
Bonlez par Grez-Doiceau, Belgium
PETER BRADFORD
New York, New York
GUNNLAUGUR SE BRIEM
Oakland, California
MATTHEW CARTER
Carter & Cone Type, Cambridge
JAMES HARTLEY
University of Keele, United Kingdom
AARON MARCUS
Emeryville, California
DOMINIC MASSARO
University of California, Santa Cruz
ESTERA MILMAN
University of Iowa, Iowa City
KENNETH M. MORRIS
Siegel & Gale, New York
THOMAS OCKERSE
Rhode Island School of Design
DAVID R. OLSON
University of Toronto, Canada
CHARLES L. OWEN
IIT Institute of Design, Chicago
SHARON HELMER POGGENPOHL
IIT Institute of Design, Chicago
DENISE SCHMANDT-BESSERAT
University of Texas, Austin
CHRISTOPHER SEELEY
University of Canterbury, New Zealand
MICHAEL TWYMAN
University of Reading, United Kingdom
GERARD UNGER
Bussum, The Netherlands
JAN VAN TOORN
Amsterdam, The Netherlands
RICHARD VENEZKY
University of Delaware, Newark
DIETMAR WINKLER
University of Illinois, Urbana-Champaign
PATRICIA WRIGHT
University of Cardiff, United Kingdom

SPACE

SHARON HELMER POGGENPOHL

WORDS IN SPACE

AN INTRODUCTION

Visible language is ubiquitous, taken for granted; it is often processed automatically rather than formally seen.

Continuing the special two part series Words in Space, these articles explore yet other themes: transubstantiation (in a secular sense), reference, transformation and freedom. A strong cultural thread runs through these essays — a glance at their images clearly reveals their approach whether vernacular or artful. Each in its own way reminds us of words in space as a cultural event.

Inspired by the keywords interaction, movement, navigation, and spatiality, the copyright, title page, and contents spreads introduce the look and feel of the design, which features expressive typography activating the compositional space.

Words inhabit the pages from every direction to enliven language. Typographic scale, position, and space provide interest and emphasis. The application is bold and dramatic and defines the spirit of both journals.

The dynamic compositions demand attention. Every edge is active. Words inhabit space from all directions, including the gutter. Typographic scale, position, and orientation change constantly throughout the design. Even with all the activity, I've not altered the authors' writing in any way. Every word appears in its entirety. I don't want to give the impression that the design was random. Every decision was calculated and mapped out. Its variety and visual changes reflect the flexibility of systems and the amount of typographic play that can come out of a uniform structure. (A simple, eight-column grid is the foundation of the design.)

Visible Language, Issues 34.1 and 34.2, are exciting layouts. Typography activates the pages for the viewer. Although the visual solution may not be appropriate for many design projects, the journals successfully demonstrate how visual form must be a direct result of the content. The text of the journals is about words in space; it deals directly with spatiality, interaction, movement, and navigation. The design actively reflects these themes. I see this design as an experiment in what a book or journal can become beyond traditional applications of type and layout. Overall, I want design to reflect and reveal content, communicating the visual and verbal information in the most appropriate and meaningful way. If this can happen expressively and challenge typical design approaches, even better.

Global Positioning System (GPS), are new tools

recording movement. As a terrestrial panopticon,

e of 'being within' that merges the personal and

y/historical ideologies in defining place. In this

ough recent examples of collaborative artworks

memory and notational traces of place reveal a

of exact individual locality. The literal recording

ucted through these projects as the visible com-

ure. Instead of constricting language to a narrow

expression/technology relationship becomes a

semantic creativity.

V I S U
A L I Z
I N G P
L A C E

Connecticut College, Department of Art
270 Mohegan Avenue
New London, Connecticut 06320
Visible Language, 34.1
Wollensak, 56–75
ajwoll@conncoll.edu
© Visible Language
Rhode Island School of Design
Providence, Rhode Island 02903

ANDREA
WOLLENSAK

Satellite technologies, specifically Glol

for naming orienting, locating and reco

Like words, places are articulated by a thousand usages. They are

GPS permits a mode of performance of

thus transformed into "variations" – not verbal or musical, but

political and questions contemporary/l

spatial – of a question that is the mute motif of the interweaving

paper, I explore these concerns throug

of places and gestures: where to live. These dances of bodies

using GPS technologies. Gesture, men

haunted by the desire to live somewhere tell interminable stories

poetics within an absolute lattice of e

of the Utopia we construct in the sites through which we pass.

of the individual's place is re-construct

They form a rhetoric of space. They are steps (dance figures), glances

munication of the movement of gesture

(composing mobile geographies), intervals (practices of distinction),

navigational-numerical space, the exp

criss-crossings of solitary itineraries, insular embraces. These ges-

new starting point for aesthetic and ser

turations are our everyday legends. They open up unpredictable

THE VISIBLE LANGUAGE OF PLACE is a myriad and inter-

spaces in an order of sites. They also play within the labyrinth of

related communication of the civic and the personal, the contem-

city signs (street names, advertising slogans, historic landmarks,

porary and the historical. Place is understood in a very individual

commercial, political or academic identities), in the same way in

way as socio-geographical perceptions become internalized as

which the voice wanders, delinquent, stubborn, through the net-

memory. Place is apprehended dualistically – with cognizance of

works of the linguistic systems, tracing pathways foreign to

distinct cartographic and topographic realities. In the naming and

the meaning of the sentences.[1] MICHEL DE CERTEAU

defining of territory, place directly comports our demographic

reality, giving us a sense of belonging to our original place, and

helping us to reify the otherness of

elsewhere.

The design driven by content, the interior spreads are unique. The sans serif typeface Thesis is used consistently for primary body copy. Each article also features a second or third typeface, including Bauer Bodoni and Trade Gothic, to create individual identities within the context of the whole. Intending to enhance comprehension, words are intentionally disrupted—they shift position, turn upside down, and run off one page onto the next.

The city represents, to many writers, a vast plurality of semantic readings of landscape,
transition and the cultural forms of capitalism. Sharon Zukin argues *"that the localism,*
or neighborhood urbanism, of the modern city has been transformed into postmodern
transitional space." In the creation of the city as cultural category, it's *"sense of place has*
succumbed to market forces. Thus, the postmodern urban landscape imposes multiple

GPS also represents an inversion

of the individual marking the outdoor environment with publicly readable expression.
With GPS, expression is realized as a spatial-temporal path marked by the   environment –
a public movement recorded as private data. GPS participates as a technology to map
'sites of resistance' (Frederic Jameson's term), helping to create personal history and to
re-orient individuals to their position in the world. In so doing, GPS is a tool in developing what Jameson describes as needed to recover these sites:

the   a new kind of spatial imagination capable of confronting the

e of   past in a new way and reading its less tangible secrets off the template of

ked   its spatial structures – body, cosmos, city, as all those marked

nal   the more intangible organization of cultural and libidinal

economies and linguistic forms.[*]

perspectives which are not only wedded to economic power but also facilitate the
'erosion of locality – the erosion of the archetypal place-based community by market
forces.'"[7] The New York project described below is an exploration of GPS re-visioning the
locality of personal significance within the context of the urban   *environment.*

LAYOUT WORKBOOK   157   profiles

ENSPACE

designers jenn visocky o'grady, ken visocky o'grady, paul perchinske

Annual reports for S.A.W., Incorporated, are important marketing pieces for Solutions at Work, a company that creates opportunities for individuals with mental retardation and developmental disabilities. Enspace, who had worked previously with S.A.W., was familiar with the organization and their need to "project a viable image and the year's accomplishments to two different audiences: businesses and the MRDD (mental retardation and developmentally disabled) community," explains designer Jenn Visocky O'Grady. The challenge was to conceive a design that appropriately balanced the corporate requirements of S.A.W. with the unique and uplifting employee stories.

The Enspace design team worked collaboratively with S.A.W., with the beginning of their process marked by inspiration. "The people at S.A.W. are our biggest inspiration—whether individuals with mental retardation or developmental disabilities who strive to make positive changes in their lives, or the folks who create opportunities for those individuals to thrive in a business setting," discusses O'Grady. With each designer contributing to design development, the conceptual direction of the annual report is two-fold: thematic and visual. "Thematically, the concept was "Cause & Effect"— a play on words that illustrated both the human services and corporate focuses of S.A.W.'s mission," elaborates O'Grady. "Visually, we wanted to produce an annual that was more booklike, something small that created a more intimate and memorable viewing experience." She adds, "Once you have the concept established, you can juggle any number of aesthetic options to deliver the message."

The configuration of letterforms on the cover of the annual report unites the words *cause* and *effect*. *Its proportion mirrors and complements the shape of the page. In addition, the covers hues are dominantly cool, yet* effect, *in a strong, warm color, rises to the foreground.*

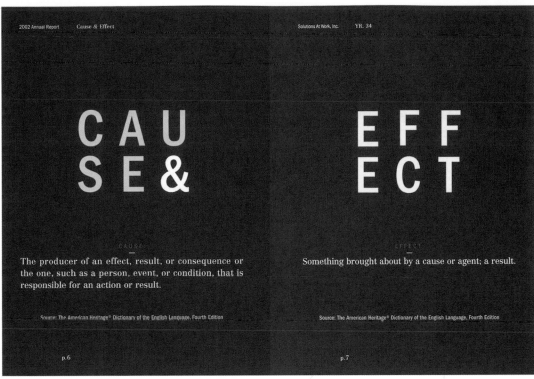

CAU
SE&

EFF
ECT

CAUSE
—
The producer of an effect, result, or consequence or the one, such as a person, event, or condition, that is responsible for an action or result.

EFFECT
—
Something brought about by a cause or agent; a result.

Source: The American Heritage® Dictionary of the English Language, Fourth Edition

Source: The American Heritage® Dictionary of the English Language, Fourth Edition

p.6

p.7

Interior spreads are simply composed. Changes in color and scale provide contrast and variation within the conservative, centered composition. Most important, this spread establishes the format of subsequent pages, which distinguishes causes and effects on the facing pages of each spread.

CAUSE

AN INTRODUCTION. A GOAL.
AN ASPIRATION.

How ever you discovered S.A.W., Inc., you are among many community members who considered the benefits of a relationship with Solutions at Work.

One of Cuyahoga County's most versatile networks, we enable our clients with mental retardation or developmental disabilities to receive specialized training in a supportive environment, increasing their independence and laying the groundwork for on-the-job achievement. The skills and motivation of our employees are certainly cause for many area establishments to utilize S.A.W., Inc.'s multifaceted, stable workforce.

Ask the business owner with a tight production schedule or the baseball team hosting a city for the evening, and they may mention a company's need to outsource at some point. We offer solutions not only customized to an employer's specific requirements, but also to the unique situations of each S.A.W. Inc. client. From the employee building her resume by learning a new computer program to a worker with perfect attendance ready for his first independent assignment, our staff proudly boasts abundant success stories of persistence, determination and achievement. Here for the individual, the employer, and our community, we remain dedicated to turning obstacles into opportunities. Why? Because as we've learned from our employees, aspiring to build a better future can be the best guarantee of a positive effect on us all.

p.8

EFFECT: ACHIEVEMENT
—
Something accomplished successfully, especially by means of exertion, skill, practice, or perseverance.

p.9

Color and scale are used consistently to order the text, which enables clear navigation through the design. A bright red hue is also introduced and effectively draws the eyes toward the dominant head on the page.

After thorough experimentation, development, and analysis, the final design is diminutive in format yet spaciously composed to easily access the content, which combines text, imagery, and information graphics. The goal to produce an intimate book is achieved "by using a loose chapter system, dividing the different sections with title pages; adding little typographic details like chapter headings, the year of the annual, and page numbers; utilizing a consistent type system; and perfect binding the piece," describes O'Grady.

The combination of a subdued color palette, accented by a sharp red hue, and classic typography creates links to the corporate environment. Serif and sans serif typefaces (Centennial and Franklin Gothic) provide consistency throughout the structured design. O'Grady continues, "Hierarchy was controlled with size contrast, color contrast (brights with dulls, lights with darks), and an underlying grid structure that provided for consistent placement and alignment, to direct the viewer's eye toward important information." Photography juxtaposes textual content and serves as a visual pause that effectively portrays the diverse personnel of S.A.W.

The S.A.W., Incorporated 2002 Annual Report competently features yearly accomplishments, while adding a human perspective that reveals the underlying strength of the organization's success. Enspace delivered their positive message in an approachable, thoughtful design.

S.A.W., INC. IS PLEASED TO RECOGNIZE THE COUNTLESS ACCOMPLISHMENTS OF OUR CLIENTS OVER THE LAST 12 MONTHS. THEIR SUCCESS IS THE ULTIMATE REASON, MOTIVATION AND CAUSE FOR BUILDING OUR ORGANIZATION. IN THE SPOTLIGHT ARE OUR EMPLOYEES OF THE YEAR FOR 2002. WE CONGRATULATE THEM FOR GOING THE EXTRA MILE ON AND OFF THE JOB. **DISCOVER HOW UNIQUE EXPERIENCES LIKE THEIRS EFFECT US ALL.**

p. 12   p. 13

An atypical interior spread provides a dramatic visual change from the conservative approach taken throughout the piece. The contrast is appealing, and the spread breaks the repetitive rhythm of the design with a bold expression. The text introduces the employee spreads that follow with a loud typographic voice that commands the attention of the viewer.

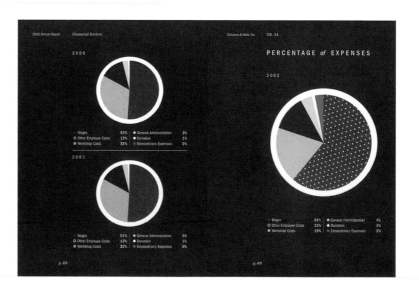

Solutions At Work, Inc.   YR. 34

CAUSE:

ROBERT "BOBBY" MATT

Parma Center
Assembly Worker
4.5 Years

Outstanding employees usually possess admirable traits like punctuality and dependability.

We also cite employees like Robert "Bobby" Matt, who chooses enrichment over subsistence with earnest commitment to realizing his potential. We are fortunate to have seen Bobby's progress at the Parma Center since transition there in 1998. Taking great pride in his accomplishments and success at work, the love of his job is reflected by Bobby's positive attitude and exceptional attendance. We recognize Bobby for being a role model with enthusiasm to try new jobs and activities and natural willingness to give it all. The success of our organization directly results from the motivation of employees like Bobby to grow, and the progress that follows.

p. 22

At S.A.W., Inc., we celebrate additional attributes, like curiosity, passion and leadership. We genuinely care about the development of our employees and their relationships in the business community.

p. 23

FINANCIAL STATEMENT

Preliminary statement of activities and changes in net income, years ending December 31, 2001 to 2002

	2001	2002
REVENUE		
Sales	6,450,227	5,166,730
Respite Program	1,688,298	1,703,447
Other	135,629	115,336
Total Revenue:	**$ 8,274,154**	**$ 6,985,513**
EXPENSES		
Cost of Revenues		
Wages	4,949,834	4,565,465
Other Employee Costs	1,064,730	929,408
Workshop Costs	1,811,600	1,398,652
Total Cost of Revenues	**$ 7,826,164**	**$ 6,893,525**
General and Administrative	296,349	294,274
Total Expense Before Donation	**$ 8,122,513**	**$ 7,187,799**
Donation Expense	60,424	52,529
Extraordinary Expense	0	191,693
Total Expenses	**$ 8,182,937**	**$ 7,432,021**
ASSETS		
Current Assets—December 31, 2002		2,746,345
Net Fixed Assets		490,147
Other Assets		3,300
Total Assets		**$ 3,239,792**

The above is a preliminary summary from the financial statements that is subject to audit.

p. 50

p. 51

Financial spreads feature simple pie charts and tables. The financial information is clear and accessible— an imperative function of an annual report.

Spreads dedicated to employees adhere to a consistent visual system throughout the design. Personal information, as well as a brief story, juxtaposes a snapshot portrait. The text on the verso page aligns on the second spatial interval of the grid. The consistency allows the viewer to recognize the ordering system quickly and efficiently from page to page.

RENATE GOKL

designer renate gokl
photographer erik gould

When I design, *I always put myself in the place of the reader and think about how*

sequence,

pacing,

A View by Two: Contemporary Jewelry catalogue was developed in support of a contemporary jewelry exhibition at the Rhode Island School of Design, Museum of Art. Cocurator Louis Mueller describes: "I hope this exhibition provides an opportunity for people to appreciate what goes into [the artists'] struggles and their creative efforts." The catalogue, which was designed by Renate Gokl, features the diverse work of fourteen international artists. "I was brought onto the project by the curator of the exhibition, a former jewelry professor of mine, who trusted that I could capture the spirit of the work," explains Gokl. "He had no specific direction for me but was hoping for something a bit unusual and nontraditional."

The jewelry was the inspiration for the design and directly affected its development. "Even though [the jewelry] was varied in terms of concept, style, materials, and technique, there was an attention to detail and perfection about the work," comments Gokl. The attention to concept, style, and detail are also evident in the design of the catalogue, which is progressive in format and typographically sophisticated. Addressing the conceptual and formal development of the design, Gokl elaborates, "The concept, one of integration and formal means, became the way of expressing it. Looking at all the material (visual and textual), it became clear that I needed to develop a system that unified the parts instead of treating them as separate pieces of information. A traditional catalogue sequence of front matter, essay, artists' works, biographies, and checklist seemed too disparate. To challenge that structure, I devised a system whereby the artists' plates and bios would group together but would also be interwoven with the essay/interview of the curator. This allowed the curator's perspective and voice to accompany the viewing of the work."

and *pauses*

might affect the experience.

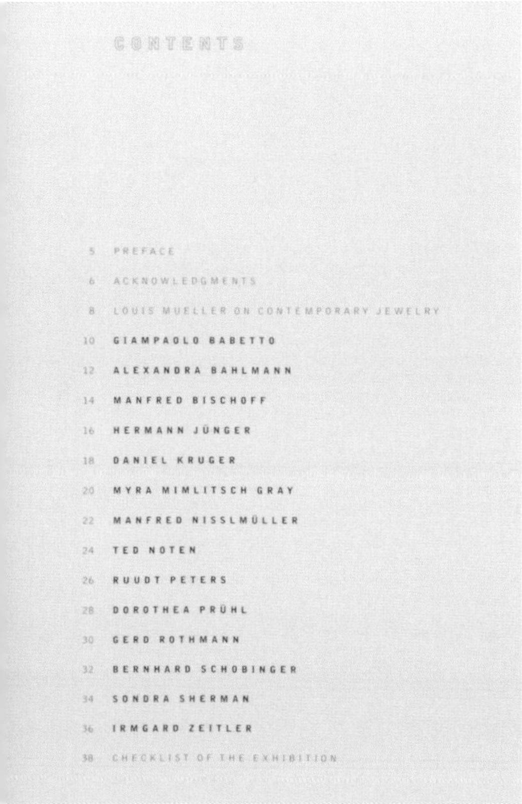

A VIEW BY TWO:
CONTEMPORARY
JEWELRY

MUSEUM OF ART, RHODE ISLAND SCHOOL OF DESIGN

CONTENTS

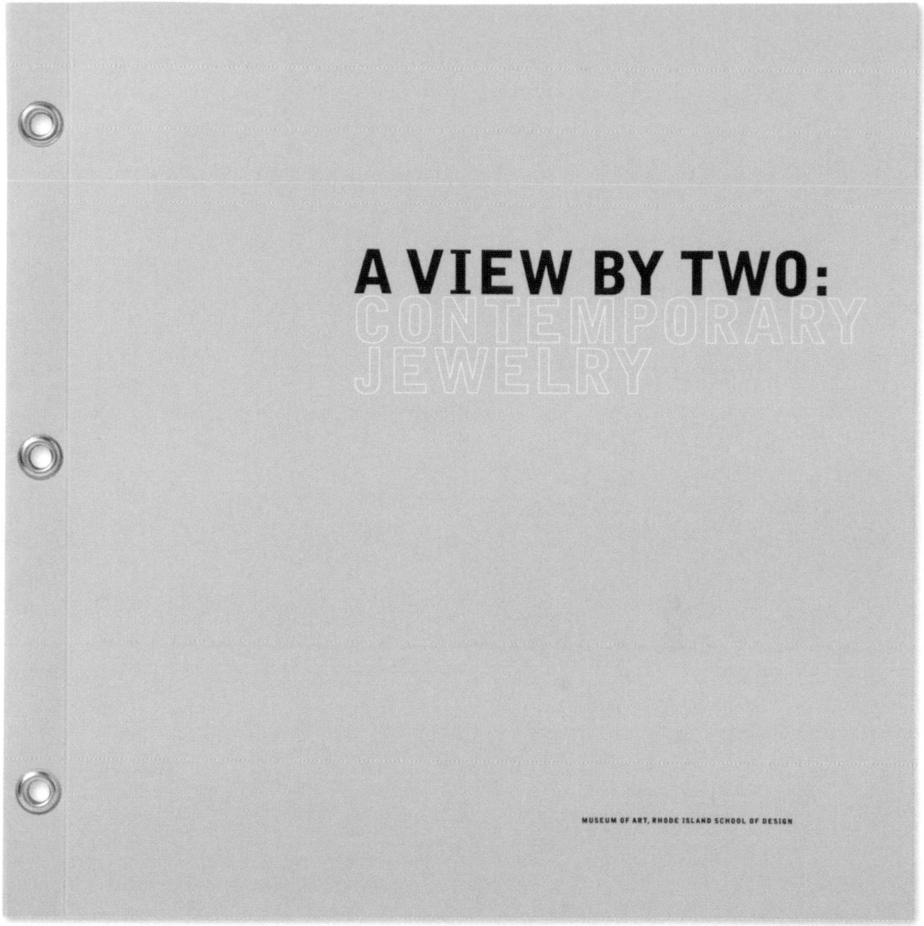

Contrasts between light and bold type weights, which are elegantly set in uppercase, create distinction between the front and back matter and the artists' names.

The asymmetric cover design commands attention through bold yet minimal typography. Appropriately spaced capitals align just above the cap height of the letterforms beneath them. Contrasting with the solid, filled black letters, the words contemporary jewelry are thinly outlined in white and suggest the delicate attention to the pieces of jewelry presented inside.

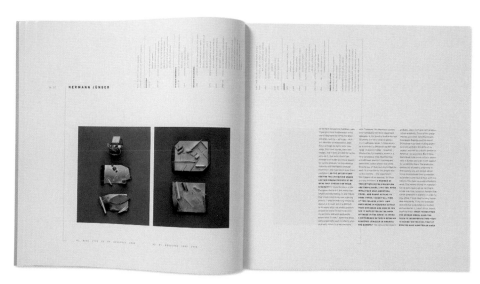

The design is built on a solid grid system that divides the page into several spatial intervals that flexibly accommodates the range of content. "A grid structure with several main horizontal alignments and five vertical columns per page helps reinforce the hierarchy," says Gokl. "The size, weight, and position of type are also keys in establishing dominant, subdominant, and subordinate relationships. Unifying the size of the images created a natural parallel between the various artists' work, whereas the formal grid structure became a scaffold upon which positive and negative space defined discrete areas of information. Also, the minimal use of a hairline rule helped articulate boundaries and groupings."

A View by Two: Contemporary Jewelry catalogue is thoughtfully presented with aesthetic skill, while serving the interests of the artists and jewelry, as well as the viewer. "When I design, I always put myself in the place of the reader and think about how sequence, pacing, and pauses might affect the experience," adds Gokl. "So, formal decisions are usually tied to functional issues." The design is avant-garde. Its form appropriately reflects its function; it effectively unifies a broad range of text and imagery in a dynamic, engaging, and artistic presentation. The sequence of the typographic presentation leads the viewer through each page, whereas the visuals of the jewelry captivate attention.

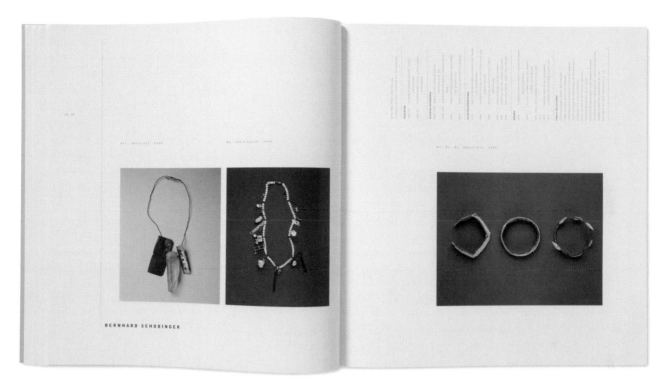

BERNHARD SCHOBINGER

Dominant horizontal flowlines dictate the starting and stopping points of the visual elements. The body text and photography share the dominant top and bottom alignment points, creating consistency throughout the design. Several vertical spatial divisions allow the widths of the photography, as well as the number of columns, to vary on each spread. Subordinate flowlines provide alignment points for biographies, names, and captions.

HAMMERPRESS STUDIO

designer brady vest

Hammerpress Studio is a letterpress and design studio located in Kansas City, Missouri. Founded in 1995 by printmaker and designer Brady Vest, Hammerpress relies on traditional, hand-crafted printing methods to create a diverse body of engaging work ranging in scope from postcards to invitations to book covers. Vest embraces and exploits the vintage art of letterpress to create tactile and dynamic visual communication experiences. Although the letterpress is certainly not a new technology or inventive style, the antiquated aesthetic is a fresh alternative to offset printing and contemporary design practice in which many designers and clients rely solely on advanced technologies to produce visual solutions.

The primary objective of the concert posters is the promotion of live music performances at a variety of venues, so the designs must provide immediate impact and accessibility to quickly send pertinent information to the viewer. Describing the initiation of the design process, Vest states, "The sources of reference and inspiration are varied, and usually, each new poster plays off the previous poster produced, as well as the anticipation of what we'll do for the next poster. For example, the Yeah Yeah Yeahs poster, as well as the New Pornographers poster, draws obvious references from Old World postage stamp graphics. However, in these pieces, there are also bits of ornamentation or imagery added that is a bit more absurd and playful."

The design process is expressive, often relying on chance and accidents to create unique, memorable pieces that, once printed, can never be re-created in the exact same way. Although the layouts are planned and systematically approached—which is evident in the strong horizontal and vertical alignment points on all the posters—the visual solutions are diverse, unpredictable, and always changing.

"Generally, the design process is 75 percent on the press," elaborates Vest. "Many decisions are based entirely on accidents, such as misaligned registrations or even illegibility. The Rocket from the Crypt poster was actually the third in a series of three posters. The first poster led directly into the second poster even though it was an entirely different concert and date. The type and ornamentation, as well as the gunfighter images, which were lifted from a collection of old pulp westerns, shifted and evolved from the first print run to the final piece. Much of this process was based on performing subtle shifts in copy, layering the colors, and allowing the posters to evolve into something interesting." Like all design projects, trusting the process is inherent—the designer is able to anticipate the outcome but is also willing to flexibly adapt to unexpected changes along the way.

The eclectic Rocket from the Crypt, Yeah Yeah Yeahs, and the New Pornographers concert posters are captivating. Capturing an aged aesthetic, each design contrasts old imagery with serif and sans serif metal and woodblock letterforms. In ordinary design applications, the diverse combinations of type and image, in addition to the decorative elements including stars, arrows, and flags, might not be as successful. The rich union of colors, graphic shapes, and typography, as well as the handcrafted expression of the letterpress, defines the posters and makes a lasting impression.

Inspired by Old World postage stamp graphics, the Yeah Yeah Yeahs and the New Pornographers posters command attention with the iconic imagery. Changes in the orientation and position of the letterforms add variety and interest to the layout, while further enhancing the eclectic flavor of the designs.

Layers of colors, patterns, letterforms, graphic shapes, and imagery establish the foreground, middle ground, and background of the poster. Visual elements are reprinted to add texture and dimension, whereas the amount of ink applied creates transparent effects. The scale of the dominant cowboy image in juxtaposition with the Rocket from the Crypt title treatments creates a strong focal point amidst the layers.

HAT-TRICK DESIGN

creative directors gareth howat, david kimpton, jim sutherland
designers jamie ellul, adam giles, david kimpton, jim sutherland
photographers richard bryant, matt stewart
copywriter scott perry

30 Gresham Street is a marketing tool for Land Securities, the largest property developer in the United Kingdom. Designed by Hat-Trick Design, the objective was to promote the sale of a prominent building to one tenant. The building, 30 Gresham Street, is located in the financial center of London, also known as the Square Mile. Because the design would be distributed to a limited number of potential tenants (only 500 were produced), high production values were a component of the design process. "Our intuition told us that to market a property in an unconventional way would appeal to the bright-minded audience, [especially] when the property market is full of off-the-shelf solutions," comments creative director David Kimpton.

The beginning of the process was marked by collaboration among the Hat-Trick Design team. "We have a brainstorm between all of us to start the design process," comments Kimpton. "We will have several of these as we progress through the initial designs. It is the most effective way of working for us and produces the best results." The results of the brainstorming sessions led to the concept for 30 Gresham Street, which "was to communicate the message

WE HAVE A BRAINSTORM

between all of us

using thirty pictures in a purely photographic book, which would sum up the scheme without the need for words. [In addition], a thirty-word brochure said it all. We provided guidebooks, such as *30 Illustrious Neighbours*, which help sell the area. It was also important to create a sense of theater from the building itself, because a large proportion of the audience would walk past it." The dominantly photographic piece is visually stimulating. Typographic content is limited yet handled classically in a combination of Helvetica Neue and Perpetua. *30*, set in Helvetica Neue, marks several elements of the design—it is iconic, branding the address. "We used the famous address of 30 Gresham Street to take ownership of 30," notes Kimpton.

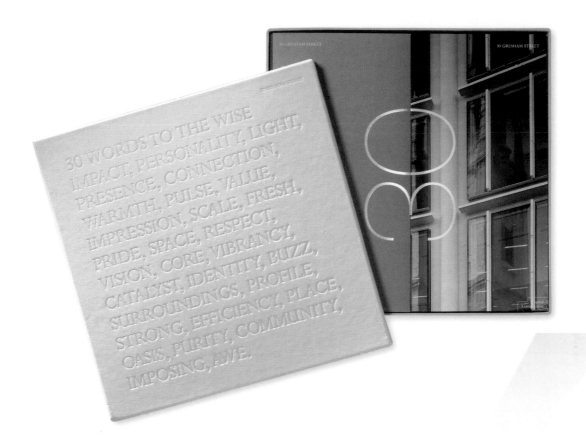

TO START **THE DESIGN PROCESS**.

Classic serif letterforms, set in Perpetua, adorn the packaging front of the marketing materials; the uppercase setting is sophisticated. The letterforms also connote architecture in their solid composition. In addition, the 30 is iconic, embodying the building in its appearance throughout the interior materials. Blind embossing furthers the refined spirit of the design.

The format of the design is distinctive and thoughtfully orchestrated. It combines all the materials into one box, and the shapes of the pieces work together to form a cohesive whole. "The building being in the Square Mile led to the inspiration for the format," adds Kimpton. "All of the literature fit in a box, which was a square foot." When the box is opened, "joint importance was given to communicating the scheme through thirty words and thirty photographs. So, the two separate books were presented side by side on top of each other." Under the two primary books lie building specifications followed by guidebooks, including *30 Points of View* and *30 Minutes Around*. The format of the elements is based on the square.

30 Gresham Street is a refined, sophisticated design that effectively promotes the property. The piece is informative and a useful reference tool. It provides detailed information about the property, as well as the surrounding area. The unique use of production techniques, including embossing and engraving, are elegant. Kimpton concludes, "30 Gresham Street has set the standard for property marketing by Land Securities and positioned them as a leader in their field."

Photography dominates as the primary communicative force of the design. The imagery visually impacts and appeals to the emotions. Intimate details of the building, as well as its surrounding environment, provide unique views that feature strong lines and angular elements. The cropped photography creates directional movement within the square compositional fields.

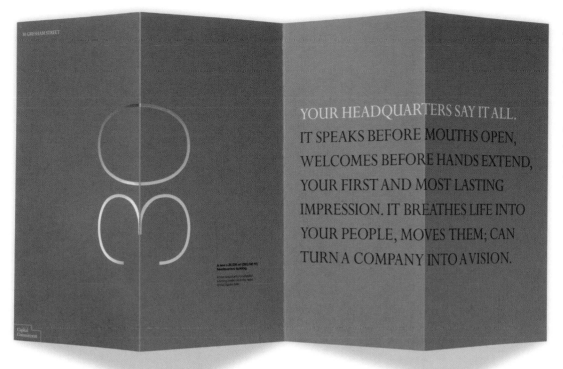

A thirty-word brochure simply states the message of the piece. The monumental letterforms command attention and complement the contemporary, foil stamped 30 that opposes it. The positive areas also reflect the horizontal format of the page. Space is used generously to activate the design and promote navigation.

The format of the supplemental pieces, including 30 Points of View, is clear and simple in presentation. Equal margins define the active space of the page, which is primarily typographic. Contrasted by full-bleed photography, or color, the text pages are composed within a three-column grid. Changes in typeface, as well as color and size, establish hierarchy.

HELICOPTER

designer ethan trask

According to their mission statement, "Theater Faction aims to set itself apart from mainstream theater practice, using unconventional and experimental methods to push theater in new directions. We will seek out the young, intelligent audience that has abandoned theater by crafting unpredictable performances in dangerous productions." *Oresteia* is the first production by Theater Faction, and the promotional materials needed to reflect an avant-garde, contemporary attitude, as well as the atypical approach taken toward *Oresteia*. Designer Ethan Trask of Helicopter explains, "Their concept for the play was [to] perform each section differently by having a different person dirɛct cach [of the three] sections." Initiating the design, which functions as a poster and program, Trask adds, "We wanted something different that spoke to a younger audience."

Inspired by "avant-garde posters and turn-of-the-century newspaper typography," the *Oresteia* poster is subjective and combines graphic shapes, imagery, and typography within rich layers to communicate messages. The viewer must interact with the design to discern the meaning weaved inside the dense, typographic composition. Discussing the concept of the piece, Trask states, "*Oresteia* is about the loss of innocence of a prince in three acts. [Also], layered within the play were a tremendous amount of pop culture references. Our first idea was to do an exquisite corpse approach, but that satisfied only the three-act quotient. We wanted to have the idea of a Greek tragedy but in a street graphic way."

Black-and-white photography provides an evocative background for the typographic elements. The image is a strong, central force and leads the eye into the lively title treatment, *Oresteia*, which is the compositional focal point. It features display letterforms turned in perspective, which adds depth and dimension. The title floats on the page and moves toward the viewer. "The headline typography came from Las Vegas neon lights and the idea of wanting to be famous," notes Trask. It is flanked hierarchically by secondary typography, including the subtitle, as well as the theater name and performance dates. Red numbers, encircled with a black stroke, label the three sections of the production and provide visual cues that guide the viewer from the top to the bottom of the composition. The poster also features multiple typefaces, including Aachen, Birch, Chevalier, and Mrs Eaves. These typefaces add contrast, diversity, and texture to the design.

The *Oresteia* poster for Theater Faction is dynamic and engaging from a distance, yet informative and revealing up close. Intriguing photography is juxtaposed with distinctive typography that composes the title, *Oresteia*, and draws the eye into the design. Upon closer examination, the design is full of typographic subtleties that allow the viewer to navigate through the two-sided composition and glean its content. It is a unique solution that makes a strong first impression for a forward-thinking client.

Helicopter conceived the double-sided Oresteia *poster and program in the innovative spirit of Theater Faction with intelligence and functionality. The hierarchically strong composition provides layers of content that are accessible and intriguing. The viewer must interact with the design to discover its graceful details, which includes the harmonious integration of multiple typefaces.*

HENDERSONBROMSTEADARTCO.

art director hayes henderson
designer/illustrator billy hackley

The American Institute of Graphic Arts (AIGA) *Boom* exhibition poster and booklet is the marketing package and awards annual for the North and South Carolina AIGA chapters. Hendersonbromsteadartco. continued the tradition (a previously used theme) and set out to create a meaningful, original design. "We chose to concentrate on the irony of the name and how it pertained to the bust economy as well as to the general climate of fear following in the wake of 9/11," explains art director Hayes Henderson. "Second, we merged this with the idea that, no matter the situation, creativity has to happen and that it can come forward even more powerfully in desperate times." The latter comment reflects the design concept that ignited the visual style of the pieces.

The *Boom* exhibition poster and booklet are the results of a flexible process from start to finish. Finessing the concept along the way, Henderson details the approach: "After creating the illustration of the figure for the poster and mailer, Billy Hackley (senior designer and concept guy on the project) and I knew we wanted to keep the piece appropriately spontaneous to match the quality of his illustration. He then looked at typography that had a similar hand-drawn feel. This developed from the initial sketch phase (the thumbnail sketches prior to going to the computer). Billy's initial comps had a fun, offbeat feel, yet they were familiar to industry people in the way they resembled thumbnail noodlings. [It was] an unusual look for an awards annual but strangely complementary to the formal presentation of the work. As well, the illustrations of the judges and other renderings were created as doodles but ended up becoming the actual artwork used."

The Boom *exhibition poster is an energetic display of illustration and hand-drawn letterforms. Both elements explode on the surface of the page and extend off its edges, yet the textural quality emits a painterly expression.*

The cover of the Boom *exhibition booklet is an extension of the poster. The illustrative* Boom *moves up the page, increasing in size as it rises off the top. Combined with a generous amount of white space, the unconventional lettering is captivating and provides the impetus to look inside.*

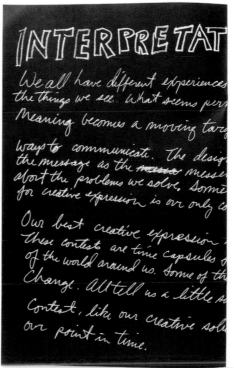

The inside front cover and title page spread provide dramatic visual contrast. Large black-and-white fields fill the composition. On the left side, a short statement, Interpretation Changes, *runs across the page and extends to the inside back cover.* Boom, *in comparison to its application on the poster and cover, is diminutive, quietly sitting along the edge of the recto page.*

Hendersonbromsteadartco. wanted to emphasize the winning design work in the *Boom* exhibition booklet. "From a layout standpoint," discusses Henderson, "we were inspired by recent design annuals that we felt had traded off proper representation of award-winning work for the designers' interest in turning the annual into a purely personal design opportunity." The oversized format is the perfect foundation of the booklet. It provides an open canvas for the spacious display of work. The limited number of examples on each page is advantageous because the viewer can carefully examine each piece. Scale accentuates the details.

The *Boom* exhibition booklet and poster feature compositional space, scale, and handcraft (illustration and typography) as their dominant characteristics. The well-planned design is loose and improvisational, yet its quirkiness leaves a lasting impression.

A typical interior spread demonstrates a clean, open composition. The visual emphasis is given to the winning design work, which is presented simply in the center of the page.

PRINT COLLATERAL
1ST

DESIGN FIRM: Black Bird Creative
CLIENT: The Brice Foundation
ART DIRECTION: Patrick Short
DESIGNER: Kristy L. Beausoleil
PHOTOGRAPHER: Scott Le Voyer
COPYWRITER: Kristy L. Beausoleil

Using varying type sizes, color, and unique, hand-drawn characters, the lettering hierarchically notes headings, subheadings, and credit information without diverting attention away from the featured work. Changing on each spread, the hand-drawn text is full of variety, from scribbled to outlined to dimensional letterforms.

the Judges
Amy Strauch, What!Design, Boston
www.whatweb.com
WWW.GRANTCOLLABORATIVE.COM
WWW.TMARKSDESIGN.COM

The judges' spread features a clever combination of illustration and photography. The imagery, framed within squares, is extended beyond its edges through the addition of illustrations that complete each picture.

YOU WILL
SEE

The Skies is a self-promotional piece that functions as an invitation and a greeting card for the design firm Hoet & Hoet. The dual purpose of *The Skies* was to send best wishes to clients while also inviting them to a festive celebration. The cards demonstrate an unusual format for an invitation and greeting card, which adds immediate interest to the design because it is an unexpected solution. The development of the piece was inspired by "beauty all around us. It was very important to show what we see each day," explains designer Véronique Hoet. "The sky surrounds us. If you turn 360 degrees, you see a different view or image of beauty with each step." The visual metaphor of the sky also communicates the hope for a prosperous future.

The imagery is evocative and carries the message of the design. The photography captures multiple views of the skies seen throughout the day—a total of fifty-five cards comprise *The Skies*. Each individual card provides a picturesque view, whereas the combination of vantage points demonstrates a range of perspectives from the solid blue sky to the setting sun. The viewer is able to see everything at once, creating a unique, memorable experience. "We forget to pay attention to the richness of the beauty around us sometimes," notes Hoet.

Typography is minimally composed on only six cards. The greeting reads, *Hoet & Hoet wishes you a clear, serene, shiny, pure, and blue 2004 and invites you under its bright new sky*. The text communicates the spirit of the cards, while directing attention toward the dominant photography. In addition, the cards are bound with a custom-made elastic band that wraps around the cards. The fluorescent color is bright and eye-catching and incites curiosity to see what it binds. The cards are also backed by bright colors that contain the Hoet & Hoet logo. The repetitive color and logo treatment unifies the cards as a set. In contrast, the backs of the cards are always changing to provide new discoveries with every interaction. "Each time and moment is different. It changes. It is never the same. It is always unique," comments Hoet.

The Skies demands interaction to experience their beauty. The cards are a constant reminder of the rich, visual environment. They surpass their practical function as an invitation and greeting card to provide a lasting impression. The positive design inspires the viewer to "go outside. Have a look. You will see wonderful things that are simple and beautiful," concludes Hoet.

WONDERFUL THINGS

THAT ARE

SIMPLE AND **BEAUTIFUL**.

Simply composed, the invitation/ greeting card features photography as its driving force. It provides visual impact while delivering the message that beauty surrounds us from all vantage points. A white border frames each image and provides a distinctive edge for viewing. Each image is a snapshot that captures beauty and time.

THE JONES GROUP

art director **vicky jones**
designer **caroline mcalpine**

The cover of the brochure is divided by a horizontal flowline that creates an alignment point along which imagery and typography rise and fall—it is the focused, active area of the design.

Geographics, a printer located in the southeastern United States, approached the Jones Group to conceptualize and design a promotional brochure that would feature their new ten-color press—one of only seventeen in the United States. "Their goal was to capture more business from the design and advertising agency community," explains art director Vicky Jones. "They wanted to position the press in a way that would dazzle designers." Inspired by the technology of the press, the Jones Group was determined to visually present the press's diverse range of capabilities to a broad group of designers. "The concept behind the brochure was to show how Geographics' new technology sets them apart in the printing business and how these advancements can directly increase the quality of work the designers create," comments Jones. "This concept shines in both the execution of the copy and graphics."

The visualization process of the brochure was led by strong writing, which outlines the theme of the design—The Geographics Difference—and clearly articulates the functions and benefits of the ten-color press. Jones elaborates, "Our goal from a design perspective was to find imagery that would capitalize on all the benefits we defined [in the writing]. The basic command Show you how… was applied in a way that outlined how the Geographics printing process helps designers set their work apart from the rest." Antique imagery ranging from fishing lures to skeleton keys to clocks was used. "Every image utilizes functions of the press that are unique to ten-color printing and not achievable by most presses," says Jones.

Photography dominates the brochure design and effectively features the capabilities of the press. It fills single pages, as well as full spreads, with each image demonstrating different printing techniques. The prominent imagery is complemented by a range of subordinate visual elements that creates a rich background of details that are noticeable upon close examination. Subtle linear elements run across the surface of the page, whereas tiny numerals knock out of the photography. Fields of colors, as well as small bars, accent several spreads and contrast with the bright white paper. Controlled typographic elements interact with the active graphic shapes, linear elements, and photography. Crop marks accent the text and simply mark the locations of headings or body copy.

The *Show Your True Colors* brochure effectively exploits the unlimited printing options available when using a ten-color press. The combination of strong, minimal copy and bold imagery clearly communicates the value and proficiency of the press. The language is focused, and the design commands attention. "The design was so effective that the brochure was reprinted a second time for client use," concludes Jones. "The Geographics sales team has come to rely on this piece to open new doors."

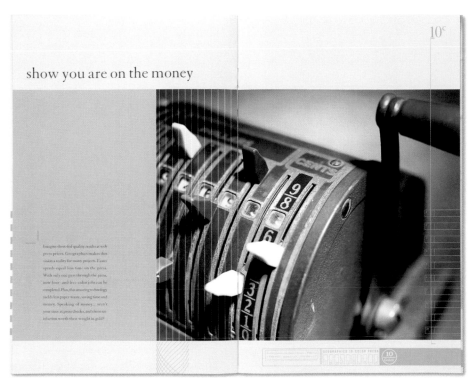

Composed within rectangular and square carriers, large photography is featured in the interior spreads of the brochure. Serif typography is set into three levels of importance: headings, subheadings, and body text. Its position is activated by the edges of the photography and linear elements. Structured lines direct the eye through the compositional space.

KANGAROO PRESS

designer ryan nole

The design of concert posters encourages unlimited visual expression. Intuition and creative freedom are inherent to the design process. The results are emotive and engaging, interpretive and unusual. The aesthetic of the posters crosses the boundary between design and fine art. Yet, like all forms of visual communication, the purpose of concert posters is the delivery of information. They advertise and promote the music scene, announcing events, locations, and times. Their function is useless if they do not impress and inform the pedestrian viewer.

The design process for *Songs: Ohia* began with an understanding of the client's needs. "In this particular case, I had worked with the artist and label enough to have a good idea of what they wanted," explains Kangaroo Press designer Ryan Nole. "On this particular occasion, I was asked to make a long, skinny poster, half the size of my normal show posters, and to print the posters two-up on the same stock that we are accustomed to using." The shape of the page is a challenge; there is limited compositional space to create a memorable design. "Because of the long, skinny format," adds Nole, "I knew it was going to be hard to get a good balance between type and image."

The inspiration for the design comes from "listening to the band for which I am creating a poster. If I don't like their music, chances are I'm not going to have an easy time designing. In turn, if I'm working for a band that I love, the poster seems to design itself," describes Nole. The next step of the process led Nole to refer to his collection of imagery. "Whenever I see an interesting image in an old magazine or book, I cut it out and store it in a cigar box," discusses Nole. "I started this design with an image of an owl that I had saved with *Songs: Ohia* in mind. The image was an old German trademark that really stuck out to me."

The screenprinting process of the Songs: Ohia *poster features black, white, and red inks printed on gray stock. The technique is rough and textural, which adds a unique impression. In addition, the designer makes use of an unusual page size by successfully complementing its shape through the vertical movement of the visual elements, such as raindrops falling down the page.*

As the dominant element of the design, the owl is the focal point that draws the viewer into the composition. In support, a large rain cloud marks the top of the page. Raindrops fall downward onto a red umbrella, which adds a punch of color without taking attention away from the owl and its typographic perch. The vertical movement of the rain complements the shape of the page and leads the eye toward the bottom of the composition. White sans serif letters sit boldly within a black field that grounds the owl and contrasts the cloud. The band name, *Songs: Ohia*, is hierarchically strong and immediately accessible. Additional content falls below the name in a smaller, thinner type size and style.

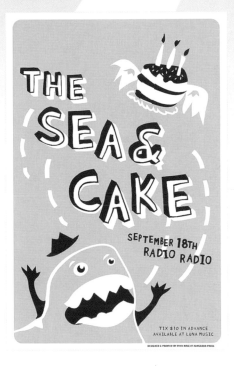

...IF I'M WORKING FOR *a band that I* **love**, *the poster seems to design itself*...

The *Songs: Ohia* concert poster presents a fresh approach toward design that is loose and instinctual. It is a reminder that design is full of expressive opportunities.

Additional concert posters feature display typography in combination with unusual imagery. The richly colored pieces are actively composed to lead the eye around the page. The band names, The Sea and Cake, Enon, and Bright Eyes, are the focal points. Their settings are integrated into hand-drawn and found illustrations, which add character to the designs. Each poster is distinct from the next, yet similar in their immediate visual appeal.

KEARNEYROCHOLL

designer frank rocholl
copywriters jesse kearney, frank rocholl

The cover designs allude to the visual system of the interior. Acting as the dominant focal point, a vertical banner of KearneyRocholl logos intentionally interrupts soft, alluring photography. The title of each piece, Daily Business *and* [Un] Daily Business, *is quietly positioned in the bottom-right corner and takes on a subordinate role to the agency name.*

The promotional books for KearneyRocholl, *Daily Business* and *[Un] Daily Business*, present a comprehensive, intelligent impression of the communications agency. The design process began by determining the best method of communicating four elements: brand theory, the agency portfolio, founder interviews, and humor. The brand theory text explains the importance of branding. The portfolio section presents the work of the agency and shares examples of their diverse capabilities. An interview provides insight into Jesse Kearney and Frank Rocholl, founders of KearneyRocholl, creating a personal connection with the viewer. Humor communicates an additional perspective of the agency. It is most evident in *Daily Business*, which presents an unusual approach toward a fabricated case study. *[Un] Daily Business* features the theory component, as well as the portfolio of work and interviews. "All in all, our approach was to show different facets of KearneyRocholl in clever, portioned parts," explains designer Frank Rocholl.

The conceptual approach toward the KearneyRocholl promotional books is motivated by the desire to cultivate a "new, unorthodox agency profile," notes Rocholl. As a result, the theme of Design Seen through Art Glasses was conceived. With this direction, "design was seen through an 'art' perspective. [The design] features funny, self-tinkered objects like Duchamp's readymades. Our logo is applied as some sort of Andy Warhol Campbell Soup assembly. A template font is used that gives [the pieces] a nondesigned charm. Sticky-tape-inspired layers run over pictures and personal statements," comments Rocholl. The design successfully combines all the divergent elements into cohesive books. Both pieces employ the same format and compositional structure, yet are differentiated by their content. Dominant typography, set in Nuri and Nuri Template (designed by Rocholl), consistently falls from the top margins. The amount of text is limited, which increases the ease of reading and allows for a generous amount of white space on the page. The typographic pages are juxtaposed with photography, graphic shapes, and type as texture, which adds dimension and interest.

HERE:
SOME OF KEARNEY AND ROCHOLL'S VIEWS
ON ╱ NOVELTY, THE DAY AFTER TOMOR-
ROW, IMAGES, BRANDS, BESTSELLERS,
INITIATIVES AND THREESIXTYNOW (?)

PLUS:
AN INTERVIEW, SOME FAVORITE ITEMS
AND MANY SAMPLES OF OUR WORK FOR
WELL-KNOWN COMPANIES.

THE DAY AFTER TOMORROW WILL NOT BE
MUCH DIFFERENT FROM TODAY. EVERY-
THING WILL REMAIN THE SAME – EXCEPT
FOR ITS APPEARANCE IN A MORE ACTUAL
VERSION.

BUT THERE IS ONE THING TO BE STRICTLY
AVOIDED IN YOUR FUTURE PLANS. DON'T
LET YOUR BRAND BECOME AN OLD
ACQUAINTANCE ╱ TOO FAMILIAR TO STIR
UP MUCH INTEREST ANY MORE.

KearneyRocholl analyzes what a brand stands for. We find ways into the future. Future compatibility. We initiate, mediate and implement communication that is clear and comprehensible. This is what we call brand activism.

╱ KEARNEYROCHOLL IS A COM-
MUNICATIONS AGENCY WITH A MARKED
COMPETENCE FOR DESIGN.

IN OUR WORK WE SET NO ARTIFICIAL BOUND-
ARIES BETWEEN PUBLICITY, DESIGN, NEW
MEDIA AND COMMUNICATIONS DESIGN FOR
FAIRS.

OUR CORE ACTIVITIES ARE BRAND UPDATES,
IMAGE AND COMPANY COMMUNICATIONS AND
CI/CD DEVELOPMENT.

OUR WORK HAS REPEATEDLY FOUND GREAT INTER-
EST WITH THE MEDIA, AND WE HAVE RECEIVED A
NUMBER OF INTERNATIONAL REWARDS.

Our references include various companies of international renown --- Audi AG, Deutsche Börse AG, Lufthansa, Toyota Europe, Guhl, Epson, Signum, Hugo Boss and smart (Daimler-Chrysler).

*Interior spreads demonstrate
a consistent application of visual
elements, including large headline
text that anchors the page. The
photography, which is encased
in dynamic graphic shapes, adds
dimension. In addition, strings
of typography are used as textural
elements. They are placed in the
color fields and on top of the
imagery to create surface depth.*

The promotional books for KearneyRocholl, *Daily Business* and [*Un*] *Daily Business*, effectively present the agency's mission and range of work, while also alluding to their personality. The design is accessible and compact, yet rich with content that is visually and verbally balanced. The books provide an opportunity for KearneyRocholl to redefine their agency and elevate their image in a smart, original way. Rocholl concludes, "We think it's always good for personal growth to torture yourself and find new ground, themes, and forms. Life is too short to be a copycat. It's interesting what happens if you have to find design solutions in an unfamiliar visual style. Anything goes these days, so let's push it."

SIGNUM / BRAND RELAUNCH, CREATIVE DIRECTION, FOTO DIRECTION, BRAND CONSULTING, EXHIBITION DESIGN, INTERACTIVE DESIGN (HTTP://WWW.SIGNUM-FASHION.DE)

EDITORIAL DESIGN / (1) AREA / INT. FASHION MAGAZINE, LONDON (2) BE / MAGAZIN OBV WINTERTHUR (3) HYPE / INT. YOUNG FASHION MAGAZINE

MÖLLER DESIGN / BRAND RELAUNCH CREATIVE DIRECTION, FOTO DIRECTION, BRAND CONSULTING, INTERIOR DESIGN, WEB DESIGN (HTTP://WWW.MOELLER-DESIGN.DE)

A portfolio spread unfolds to present numerous visual examples—the diversity and skills of KearneyRocholl are evident. The combination of exciting work with the strong text woven throughout the designs sends a powerful message. The strength of the books lies in the interaction of words and pictures.

ONE / WE FOUND THAT CLASSICAL MARKETING ENGINES OFTEN FAILED TO PRODUCE THE DESIRED RESULT.

A NEW LOGO DID NOT BRING ABOUT THE OVERALL CHANGE, SIMULTANEOUSLY EMPLOYING SEVEN AGENCIES CREATED A TOTAL VISUAL MESS, APPARENTLY IT COULD NOT BE AVOIDED THAT EVERYTHING HAD A DIFFERENT LOOK.

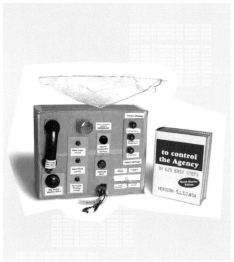

HERE:
SOME INFORMATION ON KEARNEY AND
ROCHOLL, SEVEN "FAVORITE ITEMS"

PLUS:
AN INTERVIEW / ON UNATTACHED IDEAS,
CREATIONS THAT BECAME BEST-SELLERS
AND ON KEARNEYROCHOLL AS A BRAND.

*The opening spread of the interview
section adapts the visual system and
introduces a two column structure
used for the placement of body copy.
Although the spread is textually
heavy compared to the others, it is
not visually overwhelming. Ample
column intervals, as well as spaces
between paragraphs, lighten the
impression of the text.*

FRANK ROCHOLL Born in Wuppertal. His interest in design was fostered by a friend, who wanted to become a fashion designer. Worked as Group Head Art with agencies such as Mense and Meier-and-Select. In 1993 he founded his own agency (Rocholl Projects) of Wiesbaden. Today he prefers interdisciplinary activities, working as Creative Director, Video Director and Consultant. He specializes in image- building communications and brand re-definitions.

CV Frank Rocholl took part in the development of the corporate-design and visual world of the smart car, as well as a number of publicity drives for cosmetics. He then created videos for Audi and Deutsche Lufthansa that were successfully applied at international fairs. He also published essays in specialized magazines. In 2001 he won an IDfA (Inside Design Award), in 2002 a Golden Web Award. His work has been featured in more than 50 webzines worldwide. Today he is occupied with tasks, some of them international, that require a special competence in grasping the zeitgeist.

JESSE KEARNEY Born in New York. Got round to design by way of his interest in modern architecture. He has been executive director of the exhibition and interior design agency KearneyProjects (to his core Vitalprojects) of Frankfurt/Main, extending his field of activities to include computing, interfaces, print and events. Today he works as a re-branding and communications consultant.

CV Jesse Kearney created the look of many of the dispensaries worldwide of the Deutsche Börse AG. He contributed to exhibition and fair conceptions of companies such as Hewlett Packard and Sony and has been a consultant on company communications and new fields of activities to Citibank and DRK Westanthus Verwicherung. At present he is occupied with tasks requiring keen knowledge of actual product innovations as well as a steady hand at implementing change.

THREE / THE LONG STANDING IMAGE OF THE "ADVERTISING SUPER HERO" (SEE A PICTURE OF THE MALE SPECIMEN ON THE OPPOSITE PAGE) SEEMS TO WANE.

THERE IS A CLEAR TENDENCY TO CASH IN ON THE PROMISES MADE. THEREFORE EVEN SUCH PLEASANT EXTRAS AS INVITATIONS TO DINNER AT HIGH-TONED RESTAURANTS, INCENTIVE TRIPS TO FAR-AWAY PLACES OR THAT FANCY SET OF INNOVATIVE COLOURFUL CAPPUCCINO CUPS ARE INCREASINGLY REJECTED AS A SUBSTITUTE FOR MORE SUBSTANTIAL CONTRIBUTIONS.

CONCLUSIONS / DRAWING ON THE TOTAL OF THEIR FINDINGS, THE KEARNEY/ROCHOLL COMMITTEE ON ACTUAL HANDLING OF BRANDING PROBLEMS ISSUES THE FOLLOWING RECOMMENDATIONS:

FIRST: TO STRIKE UP NEW ACQUAINTANCES CANNOT BE ALL WRONG. SECOND: IF YOU FEEL THAT SOME OF THE SYMPTOMS LAID OUT ABOVE APPLY TO YOU, CALL ON PROFESSIONAL ASSISTANCE. THIRD: A FIRST SMALL STEP MAY LEAD TO MAJOR CHANGES.

KEARNEY ROCHOLL

HELP DESK

RECODING BRANDS
CREATING IMAGES
CREATING IDENTITY

24/7

Spreads from Daily Business *introduce
humor. KearneyRocholl presents a mock
case study about the value of branding
and communication. Although the
visual system and layout is the same
in both books, stylized props (designed
by Rocholl), including The Advertising
Superhero, distinguish the books and
provide significant visual contrast to
the abstract photography and portfolio
of* [Un] Daily Business.

IDEA is

KINETIC SINGAPORE

designers leng soh, pann linn, roy poh

The packaging design for The Observatory's debut CD, *Time of Rebirth*, captures their image and sound in print. The members of The Observatory assembled after leaving previous bands. As the album title suggests, designer Roy Poh comments, "they've left the past behind to come together to be reborn again." Briefed by The Observatory to design a "distinctive" package within a limited budget, Kinetic used the title, *Time of Rebirth*, as the conceptual foundation for the design. At the beginning of the design process, "idea is always the king," says Poh.

Focusing on the theme of rebirth, the result of Kinetic's conceptualization process is the visual metaphor of a diary. Kinetic asked the singer of the band to scribble notes, lyrics, and drawings on paper to "provide an authentic look and feel" of a personal journal. With the exception of the serif typeface set on the cover of the booklet to mimic an old-fashioned diary, the typographic treatment used consistently throughout the design is handwritten letterforms.

The torn, weathered pages of the album booklet are visually expressive. They are emotional and raw. The physicality of the design is given a personal touch through the use of handwritten letterforms that list potential band names on the title page. A unique typographic approach, the alternative lettering style is used throughout the design.

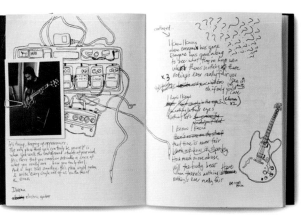

Two interior spreads feature the juxtaposition of drawings, handwritten letterforms, and photography. The visual elements add tactility to the design while communicating important content. Pictures of the band, as well as song lyrics, inform the viewer.

always the king.

The lettering "completes the personal, honest touch," explains Poh. The handwritten letterforms are imperfect, messy, and rough. As is standard in typographic application, weight is used to create emphasis. The scrawled words are written repetitively on top of each other to achieve a darker text color to define importance. An alternative to formal typography, the handwritten letterforms bring a human factor into the design.

The tactile and tattered quality of the design is linked to the theme of rebirth and blends successfully with the gritty lettering. The torn pages of the booklet represent letting go of the past to embark on a new life chapter for each band member. The gray board and wood-free paper used for the cover and interior pages are thoughtfully considered. The stock will "age gracefully and provide a richly textured feel," adds Poh. The tactility of the album packaging is enhanced through the addition of paperclips that hold black-and-white snapshots of the band in the recording studio. Like a diary, the images are moments captured in time. Seemingly askew, the photographs do not interfere with the text. The designers have composed the images to keep all the lyrics accessible. The photographs, as well as the line drawings, contrast with the letterforms and provide visual impact and further materiality to the design.

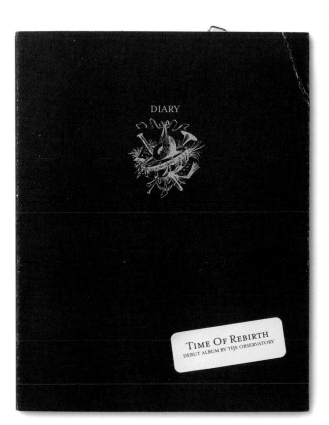

The packaging design for The Observatory's Time of Rebirth *creates a link between the viewer and the band. Through the visual metaphor of a diary, the viewer is a voyeur to the album-recording process. Kinetic creates a fitting and interesting package that is distinctive in its handmade, intimate quality.*

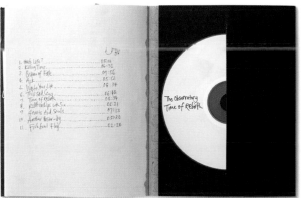

The final spread of the packaging design for The Observatory's Time of Rebirth *is a fitting conclusion to the piece. Contrasting earlier spreads, the handwritten letterforms are cleanly presented without additional notations and scribbles. The track listing is accessible and informative.*

KOLÉGRAM

designer **gontran blais**

The Opera Lyra Ottawa brochure is an elegant presentation celebrating the company's twentieth season. Designed by Kolégram, the piece successfully captures the sophisticated, yet playful, character of the opera. The design is classically composed with a hint of novelty. The contrast of tradition and modernity is thematically woven throughout the design to support the directive of the piece, which "was to create a season brochure that would attract not only the existing opera crowd but also the young, hip crowd," states designer Gontran Blais.

The conceptually driven design features refined typography and unusual imagery. "I wanted to create a look that would stand out from the rest for the company's twentieth season," explains Blais. "I also did not want to use pictures of people. Instead, I used two-dollar plastic dolls to illustrate the two major operas [*Madama Butterfly* and *Les Contes d'Hoffmann*]. I thought that the mixture between fancy and contemporary would be a good balance. Basically, my concept was mixing old with new, creating something accessible to all."

The dominant content, *Madama Butterfly* and *Les Contes d'Hoffmann*, dictates the construction of the brochure's interior. Kolégram fashions a gatefold that calls attention to the operas and adds an element of surprise. "The two major operas were the most important information in the brochure," discusses Blais. "They had to be the main event. I placed them in the middle of the brochure and worked around them." The inner page unfolds to reveal bright colors, quirky dolls, and a pair of smaller brochures lightly glued to the main page. The colors and dolls identify each opera, whereas the attached pieces provide an intimate focus.

The Opera Lyra Ottawa brochure is wrapped in a black sheet that opens into a typographically ornate poster. The treatment is dynamic— large letterforms interact and create a rich texture. In contrast to this bold expression, the minimal cover is traditionally set in a centered arrangement. A subtly tinted 20 sits behind the title, and supplementary typography falls to the bottom; a red subtitle accents the top of the page.

Interior spreads are symmetrically composed to achieve balance. Ornamented, colorful pages add visual contrast to the fixed columns of centered and justified text on the facing pages. A two-column structure is imposed to accommodate the bilingual requirement of the design.

The Opera Lyra Ottawa brochure is creatively packaged for mailing. An exterior wrapping that opens into a poster envelops the piece. Solid black on the exterior, the poster unfolds to expose a beautiful typographic texture that provides an expressive backdrop for the brochure. The piece is symmetrically composed along a central axis that is introduced on the cover. A dominant two-column structure, which features justified body text and centered supplementary copy, supports the brochure's bilingual content. Changes in type color and size in headings, subheadings, and callouts provide hierarchy.

Solidly composed, designer Gontran Blais of Kolégram transforms the Opera Lyra Ottawa brochure into a cosmopolitan design that integrates multiple levels of information into an interactive layout. Drama and wonderment begin as soon as the viewer unwraps the brochure and moves through it to see what unfolds.

The middle spread of the brochure
features a gatefold that opens to
highlight Madama Butterfly and Les
Contes d'Hoffmann. Presenting curi-
ous imagery of plastic dolls stylized
for each opera, the pages also contain smaller brochures that provide
overviews of the main attractions.
The gatefold is an unexpected, tactile gem that explodes with bright
colors and original imagery.

The *Come Forward: Emerging Art in Texas* catalogue and exhibition celebrates Texas artists "whose work is young but shows a conviction, clarity, and ambition that defy geographic borders, whose work history lies not behind but before them," describes John R. Lane, Dallas Museum of Art's Eugene McDermott Director. The exhibition catalogue, designed by Sibylle Hagmann of Kontour Design, features the artwork of a new generation of contemporary, forward-thinking artists, as well as accompanying essays by rising Texan writers. The catalogue verbally and visually presents a broad scope of creative innovation. For the design of the exhibition catalogue, the Dallas Art Museum "requested a fresh, young-looking, and, to a certain degree, experimental design—characteristics that are rather unusual for a Dallas Museum of Art publication," explains Hagmann. "Normally, the design of their books is conservative."

The cover sets the tone of the interior. The imagery is composed in vertical rectangles, which indicates the flexible grid used throughout the design. The typography adopts a subordinate role on the cover, whereas the introduction of unique typefaces adds character to the progressive design.

I had an **INTEREST** in making *the book*

The diverse presentation of artists and writers is the driving force of *Come Forward*. "One of the goals was to present each artist's work appropriately and, at the same time, establish a visual consistency throughout the book," states Hagmann. "I had an interest in making the book as lively as possible." The catalogue is structurally composed, yet adaptable, to accommodate compositional expression and variety. Its horizontal format is divided into a number of spatial intervals to support generous amounts of text, which varies from limited front and back matter to extensive essays to artists' descriptions (the most expressive typographic spreads). The spatial intervals also provide edges for artwork and fields of color that "harmonize with the widths of the text columns and sometimes don't—to create a more livelier stage," describes Hagmann.

"The established layout, grid structure, and subentities allowed for great flexibility in terms of how text and images can be arranged. I was concerned with establishing an overall skeleton structure that had enough flexibility to keep a certain order and, at the same time, allow things to be placed where, intuitionally, they felt best." In addition, the long, wide pages provide ample room for artwork featured in small and large sizes throughout the catalogue. An effective use of white space allows for ease of reading and viewing of artwork. It also directs the eye toward important areas within the layout.

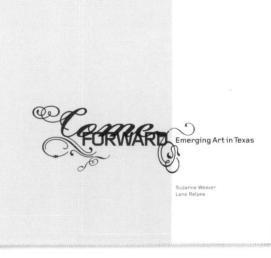

The inside front cover spread presents the consistent visual elements used throughout the design. Full-color imagery dominates. Subdued colors create rectangular fields, and linear elements outline and reinforce the grid. White space is used generously and provides an open environment that draws attention toward the title treatment.

as lively as possible.

The *Come Forward: Emerging Art in Texas* exhibition catalogue combines structure with poetic expression. The design is calculated and organized, yet also relies on the strength of the designer's intuitive sense to elevate its final presentation. "To a certain degree, part of a design process and visual solution is based on intuition," adds Hagmann. "Perhaps as a designer's experience grows, intuition becomes more and more part of the overall approach to establish the characteristics of a visual piece." Like the artwork and essays, the design of *Come Forward* is equally contemporary and forward-thinking, and, like the artists and writers, it is conceived and composed by an emerging designer.

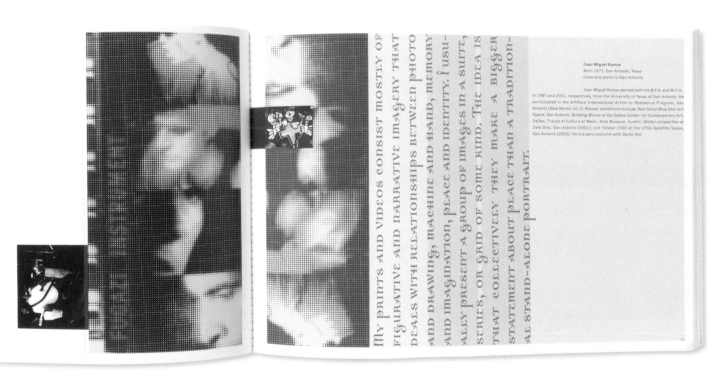

My prints and videos consist mostly of figurative and narrative imagery that deals with relationships between photo and drawing, machine and hand, memory and imagination, peace and identity. I usually present a group of images in a suite, series, or grid of some kind. The idea is that collectively they make a bigger statement about place than a traditional stand-alone portrait.

Juan Miguel Ramos
Born 1971, San Antonio, Texas.
Lives and works in San Antonio

Juan Miguel Ramos earned both his B.F.A. and M.F.A. in 1995 and 2001, respectively, from the University of Texas at San Antonio. He participated in the ArtPace International Artist-in-Residence Program, San Antonio (*New Works: 02.3*). Ramos' exhibitions include *Red Dot* at Blue Star Art Space, San Antonio; *Building Blocks* at the Dallas Center for Contemporary Art, Dallas; *Traces of Culture* at Mexic-Arte Museum, Austin; *Stolen-properties* at Sala Diaz, San Antonio (2001); and *Telstar 2000* at the UTSA Satellite Space, San Antonio (2000). He is a percussionist with *Sexto Sol*.

Display typefaces are used throughout the catalogue and are especially apparent in the artists' spreads. They establish the attitude of the design and reinforce the contemporaneity of the exhibition, as well as the forward-thinking nature of the artwork. Typography is both conservative and expressive; it actively turns on its side, changes scale, and fills the page, yet works within the defined structure.

Long, horizontal spreads accommodate large amounts of body copy. The grid provides strong edges for the placement of justified columns, which are nicely composed because the relationship of type size and column widths is considered. Fields of color are used as background elements that change in width to contrast with the shape of the columns.

LICHTWITZ

designers kriso leinfellner, stefanie lichtwitz

Lichtwitz was approached by Neubau Gastronomie GesmbH to develop a logo and flyer series promoting the Vienna music club, Europa, Hinterzimmer. To initiate the project, "we usually try to start an efficient design process with conceptual and strategic considerations," explains designer Stefanie Lichtwitz. The design was influenced by a limited budget, as well as time restraints. "Flyers often must be produced on very short notice," states Lichtwitz. In addition, Lichtwitz would not be the sole designers for the flyer series. A logical, visual system needed to be established that would foster brand recognition and usability by different designers and nondesigners. "Some [events] are organized by external organizers who work with third-party designers of their own choice. If so, the club should be easily recognizable in each flyer, even when a completely different visual language is being used," notes Lichtwitz.

The visual direction of the Europa, Hinterzimmer logo and flyer series is inspired by the architectural details of the club, as well as "the lively, creative music and DJ scene." The circular logo "evokes [the shape of] a keyhole, because the name of the club, Hinterzimmer, literally means 'back room,'" adds Lichtwitz. The flyer series is shaped like a cassette tape. It is characterized by rounded corners, which soften the edges and relate to the shape of the logo. "We took the typical mix-tape produced by DJs as an analogy. They often come in packaging that is handcrafted in a personal and artistic way with the typical format of a cassette box [being] the only constant," says Lichtwitz. To standardize the flyer series, the logo is die cut into each piece. It is the focus of the flyers, a consistent brand identified with all club events. Although the logo size remains the same, its position changes on each card, which provides flexibility in the application of the visual elements.

The logo and rounded corners, which remain constant elements, "built the framework for all the flyers," comments Lichtwitz. A flexible system "focused on a small set of fixed components" allowed others to work easily with the format. Lichtwitz elaborates, "We did not want to come up with too many rules [and] restrict third-party designers in their contributions." The changing styles of the flyers are dynamic, experimental, and interesting. "Some flyers are designed in our office and offset-printed in large quantities. Others are based on preproduced blanks that were customized by hand with stickers, rubber stamps, tags, stitching, or hand drawings by DJs or organizers," discusses Lichtwitz. "It was amazing to see the diversity of ideas and designs that these external 'design amateurs' came up with."

The Europa, Hinterzimmer logo and flyer series is fresh and innovative. It allows designers and nondesigners to create and share visual ideas. "The variety of flyer designs reflects the inventiveness and agility of the Viennese music scene well," concludes Lichtwitz. "We learned that many customers have started to collect the flyers."

The consistent shape, as well as the die cut logo, defines the visual system for the flyer series. Each flyer is unique and customizable, demonstrating a range of designs that incorporate abstract photography and texture. The range of examples is varied, yet they remain connected because of the visual markers that tie them together.

Additional handcrafted flyers feature the diversity of solutions available. They also serve as inspiration for club organizers to design their own flyers in the future. By keeping the visual system flexible, creative and expressive compositions dominate.

MITRE DESIGN

creative director troy tyner
designers john foust, kevin pojman, elliot strunk, troy tyner
copywriter julie curtis

The eclectic design of the poster is magnetic. Comprising four pieces, the poster is cohesive and demonstrates diverse compositional solutions. A range of typographic treatments includes hand lettering contrasted with computer type. The surface textures are rough and smooth; the colors are bright and subdued. In addition to its visual impact, the function of the design ignites a call-to-action— it is a positive campaign that builds the local community.

Classic Graphics, a printer located in the southeastern United States, initiated a poster project with a number of regional firms. The content of the posters was to be determined by the participating designers; each firm became their own client. The opportunities for communication and visual expression were endless. Seeking inspiration in their "own backyard," Mitre Design chose to maintain and cultivate local ties within their community "to help others understand that everyone plays a vital role in building a healthy, well-rounded 'hometown' by supporting the areas that form the unique fabric and culture of our local community—music, theater, art, and trade," explains creative director and designer Troy Tyner. The initiative developed by Mitre Design, Make a Scene, is "a citizen call-to-action."

To reflect the areas of music, theater, art, and trade within one design, the poster was divided into four smaller pieces. Each quadrant focuses on one of the cultural areas. "The process was one of total collaboration by our designers," states Tyner. "Everyone worked independently to contribute ideas before we all came to agree on the best direction. Each designer had a specific view and emotional connection to what we were addressing." With the concept and format established, the designers sought visual inspiration. Tyner discusses, "Stylistically, our inspiration was drawn from many areas. Each mini-poster needed to speak in the visual vernacular specific to the cultural venue used to communicate the message (that is, music, theater, art, trade). So, our sources of inspiration were found in posters, bills, flyers, and so on, from similar venues—both historic and more current examples. The challenge was to create a look that was an immediate read without directly cribbing a style— or designing a cliché."

EACH POSTER
IS *DISTINCT*, YET
THE MESSAGE
IS *CONSISTENT.*

The design of the poster is diverse, with its visual elements ranging from rough textures and hand lettering to ornate patterns and computer-generated typography. The color palette is equally diverse yet balanced, which prevents any of the four pieces from dominating the others. (Although the poster works successfully as a single design, it contains perforated lines that allow the quadrants to be separated.) "Each poster is distinct, yet the message is consistent," notes Tyner. The viewer is provided with a dynamic visual expression that is immediately engaging and requires interaction with each section to understand its meaning. "At a glance, they read as they should and draw the viewer in. It's only when you read further that the true message is delivered," comments Tyner. "This is one of those cases where the look of the piece took front seat."

Beyond the commanding aesthetics, the message of the poster is most significant. The effectiveness of the Make a Scene poster has "expanded to additional offline marketing materials, special events, and a soon-to-launch community website," adds Tyner. The awareness brought to the local community, as well as the encouragement to participate within it, is the strength and success of the design.

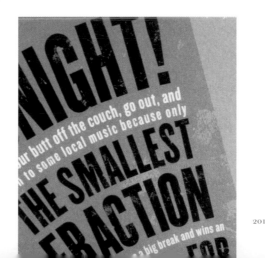

NB: STUDIO

photography martin morrell

The *Jerwood Applied Arts Prize: Glass* marketing materials demonstrate a consistent visual system that combines basic elements—color, photography, and typography—to create a unified series, including a poster, catalogue, and invitation. Designed by NB: Studio, the materials promote an exhibition that features the work of glass designers. "We were looking for something that would talk about the interaction of glass and designer without showing a designer," explains NB: Studio's Alan Dye. "Usually, in an exhibition like this, the designer or curator chooses an iconic example that sums up the spirit of the show and becomes the marketing image. We knew that a prize was going to be awarded to one of the exhibitors later on, so we couldn't justifiably feature any single person's work in the material."

The inspiration for the design came from the work featured in the exhibition, as well as the medium of glass. "Clearly, if you can see any of the work for real, this will provide the most inspiration," adds Dye. "[And], glass is so flexible a medium. It can be made to look painfully delicate or amazingly solid. It can be crystal clear or black as night." Experimentation was the key to a productive design process. "We decided to do our own experiments, so we bought some glass from a local glazier and started to mess around with it, [including] layering, breaking, scratching, and shining light through it," comments Dye. "Inspiration came when we noticed a door in our studio had a window above it made from fluted glass. This stuff is great. It distorts what is behind it in a vertical, compound-eye way. We decided to order a large piece of this fluted, or readied, glass and photograph someone acting as a designer/craftsperson behind it. Now we had our image of material and human interaction."

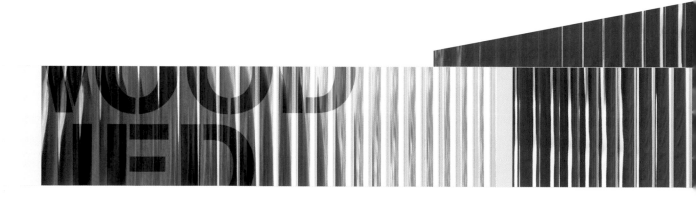

JERWOOD APPLIED ARTS PRIZE 2003 GLASS

21 August to
5 October 2003

Crafts Council Gallery
44a Pentonville Road
London N1 9BY

Free Entry
Tuesday to Saturday 11–6
Sunday 2–6 Closed Monday

Disabled Access &
www.craftscouncil.org.uk
3 minutes from Angel
Telephone 020 7278 7700

Alexander Beleschenko
Katharine Coleman
Matthew Durran
Amber Hiscott
Angela Jarman
Helen Maurer
Colin Rennie
Koichiro Yamamoto

An abstract photograph activates the poster. Although abstract, the image is also very graphic. The impression of the glass creates long, vertical lines that create alignment points for the placement of typographic elements.

The catalogue introduces an additional abstraction of the primary image used on the poster. The compelling visual effect attracts the viewer. As a result, supplementary information is not needed—the photograph serves the communicative function of the design.

With the dominant photograph established, the communicative function of the imagery was enhanced with the addition of typography. Geometric, sans serif letterforms contrast with the abstract photograph. They provide not only a solid field that commands attention throughout all the pieces but also the leading edge for the alignment of subordinate typographic elements on the invitations. "We chose a stencil font based on Akzidenz Grotesk as our typeface for the job. It seemed appropriate as a display font. It was bold and easily legible," comments Dye. "Taking the title of the show as our most important message, we used it huge on the poster in upper-case because it had to stand out of our complicated image." All the pieces consistently incorporate the title treatment to unify the system.

Striking photography is combined with strong typography to create an exciting visual impression of the *Jerwood Applied Arts Prize: Glass* materials. The final pieces "successfully capture the overall feeling of the exhibition," concludes Dye. They are the result of visually exploring and interpreting the quality of glass—experimentation yields powerful results.

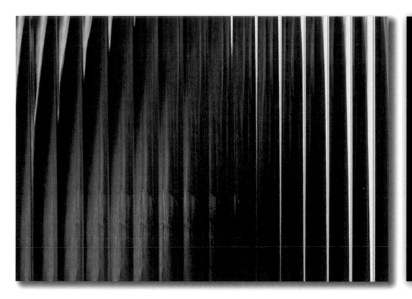

The bold, typographic title treatment
on the exhibition invitation creates
impact. The emphasis on the word
glass *easily identifies the exhibition
theme. The contrast of white on
black is also effective. The opposing
side features a dynamically cropped
abstraction of the poster image
that establishes the color palette
of the design.*

The award ceremony invitation
mirrors the layout of the exhibition
invitation, introducing materials
that connote the transparency of
glass. The linear markings on the
transparent paper reflect the
vertical lines in the photograph.
It is the evolution of the pieces
that references and reinforces
the original image.

NOON

creative director cinthia wen
designer ellen malinowski
photographer rj muna

The collateral materials for ODC/San Francisco, designed by Noon, bring dance alive. The presentation is dramatic—it captures the expressiveness of dance throughout the range of pieces, which include a booklet, invitation, and postcard. "The campaign solution needed to visually represent the choreography, program, and company as a whole," explains creative director Cinthia Wen. "In addition, it had to be produced within a tight time line, with strict production parameters and a limited production budget." Understanding the needs of ODC/San Francisco was imperative. Noon met with them to discuss the project, as well as the objectives of the dance season. Wen elaborates, "We attended ODC's season performances in 2002, as well as work-in-progress performances and discussions throughout the year, to further our understanding of the company. We also attended performances of other dance companies to pinpoint ODC's uniqueness. Through the process, we learned what should be emphasized—the essence of ODC's choreography, stands, and poses to create a static composite that captures the energy of the live performance and represents the company as a whole."

The "energy, fluidity, and grace" of the dancers and performances inspired the design. Dramatic photography provides a unique opportunity to observe the spirit and physicality of dance. "Respecting the work of the photographer was one of our main concerns," says Wen. "RJ Muna is a fantastic artist. The final piece is as much of an attribute to his talent as it is to our design." The collateral materials feature dancers on every page with their striking poses frozen in time. The photography heightens the strength of the dancers and vividly demonstrates the manipulation of the body. It intensifies every move and communicates the essence of ODC/San Francisco.

Emphasizing the motion of dance, the collateral materials exhibit "visual impact followed by information hierarchy," notes Wen. The arrangement of the photography on black-and-white surfaces elevates it as the dominant visual element. It is complemented by clean and sophisticated typography. Using the typefaces Mrs Eaves and Trade Gothic, the typography is composed around the active photography. It fosters clear communication of the content, including dates, locations, and performances. Changes in case, as well as color, position, and scale, add dimension and hierarchy. The contrast of the evocative imagery and typography provides a spacious environment throughout the materials.

The collateral materials for ODC/San Francisco are strong, visual expressions. The design captures dance while effectively communicating content. Reflecting on the final design, Wen concludes, "Dance is a unique form of art. One can discuss the form of dance intellectually as much as one can and it still would not compare to the real thing. As helpful as finding brand attributes and characteristics can be, the standard strategic analysis does not apply when it comes to performance art. The design for the final piece is ultimately from the gut, in response to the performances and to what was captured in the photography. It is incredibly visceral."

IT IS **INCREDIBLY** *VIS*

The ODC/San Francisco collateral materials include a brochure, invitation, and postcard. The visual system features striking photography that activates the page and captures the intensity and beauty of dance. Imagery dominates the design—it is the primary focal point that attracts the viewer into the compositions.

C E R A L.

NO.PARKING

designer elisa dall'angelo

Riadruck is a fabrication and production company whose
work ranges from die cut lettering to digital printing to sign
manufacturing. No.parking was approached by Riadruck
to design a catalogue that would reflect the diversity of the
company's services. Designer Elisa Dall'Angelo explains
further: "[The catalogue] should inspire new clients who
work in the design business (graphic designers, architects,
interior designers) and support them to get their ideas to
work." A difficult challenge, the next step was to determine
how to "show all [of the services] in a catalogue, get a logical order into it, show real printing examples, and give the
whole lot a strong image," adds Dall'Angelo. An additional
consideration was flexibility, which was essential to allow
the materials to be updated without a complete redesign.
According to Dall'Angelo, "the only important thing for
the client was that the catalogue had to offer the possibility
to add or take out folders."

*The exterior of the catalogue
introduces the viewer to the
clever comparison of fruits and
vegetables to fabrication and
production services. The lettuce
is a simple, eye-catching image
that establishes the visual
symbolism for the product information lying inside. The cover
also establishes the visual
system that is echoed inside
of the catalogue.*

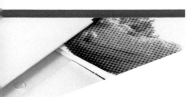

The design process began with the development of a unique metaphor. "We wanted to show the multiplicity of the company's products using fruits and vegetables to give a positive feeling," states Dall'Angelo. For example, a tomato represents big prints; a melon signifies digital prints. Other fruits and vegetables incorporated into the design include lettuce, peppers, and strawberries. "They gave a fresh and colorful look to the company and are neutral objects that could be used to show different printing techniques," comments Dall'Angelo.

The catalogue features a bright, fresh color palette based on the shades of the fruits and vegetables featured. Although a diverse range of hues exists, their vivacity ties the package together and connotes a friendly, positive attitude.

No.parking established a straightforward visual system "by using the images of fruits and vegetables and strong colors combined with big numbers," says Dall'Angelo. The visual impact of the photography directs the viewer into the structured compositions. Large fields of color (determined by the hue of the fruit or vegetable) counter the imagery, dividing each of the individual pages into halves. The range of shades is also evocative and vivid when the catalogue is viewed as a whole. Textual content is logically ordered throughout the design to achieve clarity. Large sans serif numbers create a typographic focal point that is followed hierarchically by a heading and tertiary descriptive text.

No.parking uses metaphor to establish the thematic foundation of the appealing Riadruck product catalogue. The playful symbolism of fruits and vegetables successfully parallels the diversity of services offered by Riadruck. The final design combines clear communication with an energetic, stylish image.

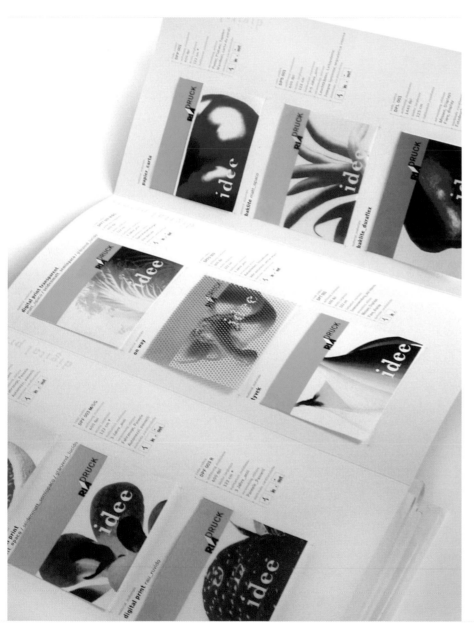

Interior pages open to reveal product samples and specifications. The layout is composed in an orderly fashion to provide emphasis on the printed swatches, yet allows for product comparisons across the spread. The viewer can see everything at once and easily access information.

No.parking designed a systematic structure to lay out the loose pages of the catalogue. Although the fruits, vegetables, and color change on each cover, the basic method of spatial organization remains the same. Dividing the page in the horizontal center, imagery falls to the bottom of the composition as typography rises to the top.

PETRICK DESIGN

art director, copywriter robert petrick
designer tracy west
photographer tom maday
illustrators tim tomkinson, friend and johnson

Domtar approached Petrick Design to develop a paper promotion that would position them as an educator and become a reference tool for designers and printers. The results are the Domtar Answer Packs, a series of cards (collated and bound by subject) that explain and illustrate different printing techniques while promoting the range of Domtar papers. Some of the questions addressed in the Answer Packs—including the titles *On Color*, *On Dots*, and *On Texture*—are: What's the difference between varnish and coating? How do you get stunning effects using color ink on color paper? What happens when you emboss an embossed sheet? The design approach began "with research, word mapping, and brainstorming," comments art director Robert Petrick. "We make sure we clearly understand the audience, the product we are selling, and the competitive landscape."

The Domtar Answer Packs were inspired by "old-fashioned flash cards that are used to teach children how to spell," notes Petrick. Taking the inspiration a step further, Petrick discusses the project's conceptual development: "[The Domtar Answer Packs are] a series of packs issued periodically and assembled over time to create a reference library of design, printing, and paper techniques. Each pack is limited to a precise and focused topic so that each one is covered in depth. The cards remain loose [unbound] so that comparisons between cards are easy and effective. The backsides of the cards have a narrative presented in storybook form, which is fun and fantasy-like and provides subject matter for the visuals on the front or demonstration side. The hero of each narrative is named in alphabetical order and alternating genders, the same way hurricanes are named. The models for each photo are actual Domtar employees."

With the idea thoroughly conceived, the size of the Answer Packs was determined based on other products in the Domtar line. "The cards ended up being the same size as the Domtar swatch books so they could be kept, in theory, on the same shelf," says Petrick. Hierarchically, "because the image is the information in this context, it made sense to make the image dominate each card. The card number is also important, because we reference it constantly when discussing card comparisons," explains Petrick. "We ended up imposing further structure onto the content by separating it into sections, or chapters." The typographic content is logically ordered and consistently set in a flush left alignment, whereas the imagery is evocative and informative throughout the series.

The Domtar Answer Packs demonstrate a strong, harmonious union of writing and design. The design is educational and resourceful yet aesthetically strong and classically composed. "The design, on a broad level, positions Domtar as a valuable resource for technical information and inspiration," concludes Petrick. "On a more practical level, it enables the Domtar sales force to present examples of how to use the wide variety of colors and textures available in the Domtar grade offering."

A visual system unifies a series of cards that features a range of paper grades and production techniques. Consistent margins, typographic settings, and position of the visual elements extend throughout the series and tie everything together. Though there is a great deal of information to review, the design is not complicated. It is approachable and accessible because of its simple elegance. The visual activity of the imagery is balanced by the simple and clear typographic presentation.

RICK RAWLINS/WORK AND VISUAL DIALOGUE

designers rick rawlins, fritz klaetke, ian varrassi

Clements Horsky Creative Directions, a print production management firm, presented the design firms Rick Rawlins/ Work and Visual Dialogue with a two-fold design problem. First, their name was confusing and demanded reconsideration; it was unclear what type of services Clements Horsky Creative Directions offered. Second, "their communications materials had an amateurish and haphazard look, which was inappropriate for a company that handles print production issues for designers," explains designer Fritz Klaetke. Rick Rawlins/Work and Visual Dialogue collaborated on the project, which began with the development of a new name for Clements Horsky. "Playing on the four-color process inks common in printing, as well as the process of design and print production, we gave the company a new name—Process," adds Klaetke. Once established, Rick Rawlins/Work and Visual Dialogue worked independently to explore visual solutions before coming together for the final concept.

The inspiration for the Process letterhead system was "the production process itself—terminology, grids, specifications, colors, and so on," comments Klaetke. The inspirational motifs would become the actual visual elements of the design—the grid and specifications are apparent in the end result.

Structurally, the letterhead system is innovative. "The entire stationery system—letterhead, window envelope, and business card—is constructed from a single sheet of 8 1/2" x 14" (21.6 x 35.6 cm) paper. The complexity of these shared functions, as well as the array of production techniques used to accomplish them, becomes a Process case study that requires careful attention to detail— details that are revealed in the fabrication specifications imprinted on the reverse."

The ingenious design of the Process letterhead is methodic. The color palette—cyan, magenta, yellow, and black—is used interchangeably throughout the system. The bold, simple company logotype, Process, is the dominant element of the design. Set in Helvetica Neue, it commands the top of the letterhead, as well as the back of the business card, which is perforated out of the 8 1/2" x 14" (21.6 x 35.6 cm) sheet. The contact information, also set in Helvetica Neue, is treated in an uppercase, flush left presentation. Color is used to distinguish information within the setting. Additional yellow text appears on the back of the letterhead and notes the specifications that describe the production of the design. For example, "letterpress score for fold at 97/8" (25 cm) from top," "10% screen of cyan for address field," and "process solid for security envelope." Klaetke adds, "This design was very systematic and rational because the process is very direct, factual, detail oriented, and precise."

Detailed views of the letterhead system feature the front and back of the business card, as well as an example of the production specifications on the back of the letterhead (opposite page). Uppercase settings in different weights of Helvetica Neue are consistently applied. The color palette is based on the four primary printing colors: cyan, magenta, yellow, and black. It is used flexibly as color fields, while also calling attention to dominant textual content.

PROCESS CORP. CREATIVE PRODUCTION MANAGEMENT
MAIL 410 GREAT ROAD BOX B3 LITTLETON, MA 01460
DELIVERY THE LITTLETON MILL BLDG 1 FLR 2 RM 3
T 978 486 0301 F 978 486 0901 C 617 899 0585
E VICTORIA@PROCESSCORP.NET
VICTORIA KAPSAMBELIS VP OPERATIONS

The Process letterhead system is clever and engaging. Rick Rawlins/Work and Visual Dialogue dramatically transformed Clements Horsky Creative Directions into Process. The letterhead system reflects their services in an appropriate and inventive format. "Bottom line: Sales increased 20 percent after the redesign/rebranding effort," concludes Klaetke.

All of the pieces of the Process letterhead system are constructed out of an 81/2" x 14" (21.6 x 35.6 cm) sheet. The innovative design appropriately reflects a company dedicated to print and production issues. The business card, perforated out of the letterhead, folds onto itself to form the envelope. In addition to the format, typographic elements are thoughtfully composed within an evident grid structure that provides vertical and horizontal alignment points for the logo and contact information, as well as production specifications on the back of the letterhead.

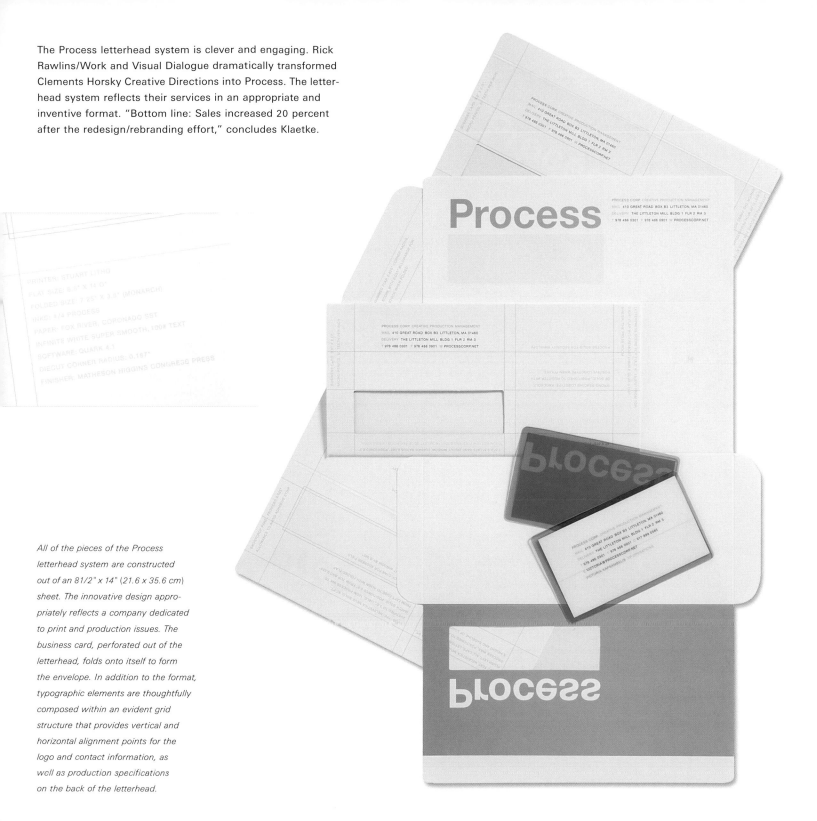

RMAC was approached by Lisbon's premier nightclub, LuxFrágil, to design a party invitation celebrating the launch of Absolut Vanilia in Portugal. "The challenge was to create a piece that mirrored the graphics and style of the Absolut Vanilia bottle without compromising the originality of the project," explains designer Ricardo Mealha. "We wanted to be original and not copy any previous ideas. So, we researched materials that would convey the message in an innovative way [and] reinter-preted the elements (bottle, textures, colors, flavor) of this particular type of vodka." The unique materials, which include acetate, fine papers, and vinyl, are tac-tile. The invitation engages the senses and reflects the essence of Absolut Vanilia.

Inspired by the Absolut Vanilia packaging, the conceptual direction of Absolux is related to the themes of "trans-parency and ice." The aesthetic objective is "a graphic style that relates to the mood and spirit of the country of Sweden," states Mealha. Reflecting the themes, the distinctive feature of the invitation is the integration of materials. "We used different materials that conveyed the key elements of this particular vodka, [while] all related to the colors of the bottle," adds Mealha. The rich materials are introduced with the envelope, which is a cool, white tone with an unusual "velvety texture." A silver-foil LuxFrágil logo and address block rest on the left edge of the envelope. The metallic color reflects the design of the Absolut bottle, which is capped with a silver top.

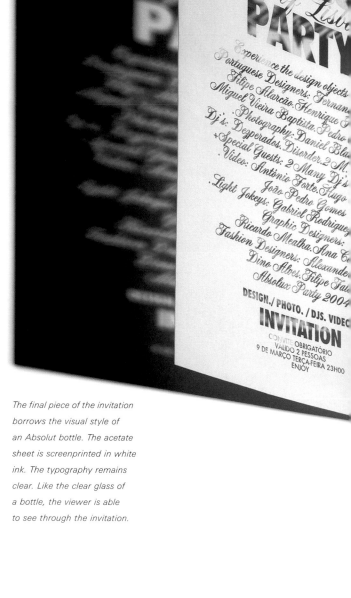

The final piece of the invitation borrows the visual style of an Absolut bottle. The acetate sheet is screenprinted in white ink. The typography remains clear. Like the clear glass of a bottle, the viewer is able to see through the invitation.

LUX

Ab. Infinite D. Arsonigo. Moreina A
Cua do Polvo e io Aplenta
1950-176 Jalna

On the interior of the envelope, three pieces are folded inside of each other. The first piece is a large white sheet with an oversized photograph of vanilla pods that opens to reveal mirror paper printed with vanilla orchids. The reflective surface is glamorous and seductive, whereas the scale of the imagery provides a unique viewpoint. The photography of the vanilla pods and orchids is natural and refreshing, suggesting the purity of the vodka. Inside the mirror sheet lies a "giant, transparent vinyl sticker that is silkscreen printed in white with the name of the participants of the project, an illustration of the vanilla flower, and the Absolut Vanilia logotype," explains Mealha. The sticker unfolds and contains the third piece of the invitation—a single acetate card also printed in white. The typographic application imitates the graphic style of the Absolut Vanilia bottle by modifying the sans serif logotype and script body text.

The journey through the Absolux invitation is ethereal. It takes an existing object, the Absolut Vanilia bottle, and adopts its graphic style. The invitation is translated into a fresh design suited to its function. The interesting use of materials, as well as the act of unfolding the piece, is interactive and mysterious—the materiality of the invitation dramatically affects its presentation.

The envelope of the invitation connotes sophistication. Its smooth texture is imprinted with elegant, silver-foil typography. The contemporary sans serif LuxFrágil logo contrasts with the script typeface. The geometry of the letterforms of the logo counters the fluidity of the linked script. The logo and address block rest quietly along the left edge, optically centered. The first impression of the invitation is a close-up view of vanilla pods. The image is abstract— its rough texture and angular composition counter the quiet tone of the envelope.

The use of material is the dominant element of the design. A sheet of mirror paper is juxtaposed with a vinyl sticker; the tactility of each piece is unique. The invitation relies on illustration and photography. Rather than using words, the imagery effectively connotes nature and purity through its visual impression. A large image of vanilla orchids fills the mirrored sheet, whereas an illustration of the flower commands the background of the vinyl sticker.

SAMATAMASON

art director greg samata
designer goretti kao
copywriter bill seyle

Seyle: Words is a promotional book for writer Bill Seyle that relies on the words and their typographic composition to intrigue and gain new clients. The design problem presented to SamataMason was "to create a book that presents a writer's work in the same way a photographer would present a portfolio of photographs," comments designer Goretti Kao. "We knew the writer well and wanted to design the book so that it represented his personality and style." The refined, letterpress book captures the spirit of the writing, which is given full attention. The typography commands interest and fosters a high level of readability within the spacious, compositional environment. Kao adds, "We knew from the start that the book should be simple and elegant without being too flashy or corporate looking."

Inspired by the writings of Bill Seyle, SamataMason "wanted to create a piece that was typographically driven, like a book of poetry. The concept was to let the writer's work speak for itself, without explanation," describes Kao. "Each piece of writing became unique in its own way and depended on the typography for personality. Because each piece needed to work independently, as well as part of a whole, we designed the book using one typeface [Bembo] in various sizes and styles. We wanted the reader to react just by looking at the type design." Italic, small capitals, and roman fonts, as well as slight changes in type size, are used to achieve typographic color, contrast, and variety.

Seyle: Words *is a beautiful typographic design. The title is composed in the top-right corner. Its position near the edge of the page directs the viewer into the interior spreads. In addition, the placement of the text establishes the consistent location of all headings within the book.*

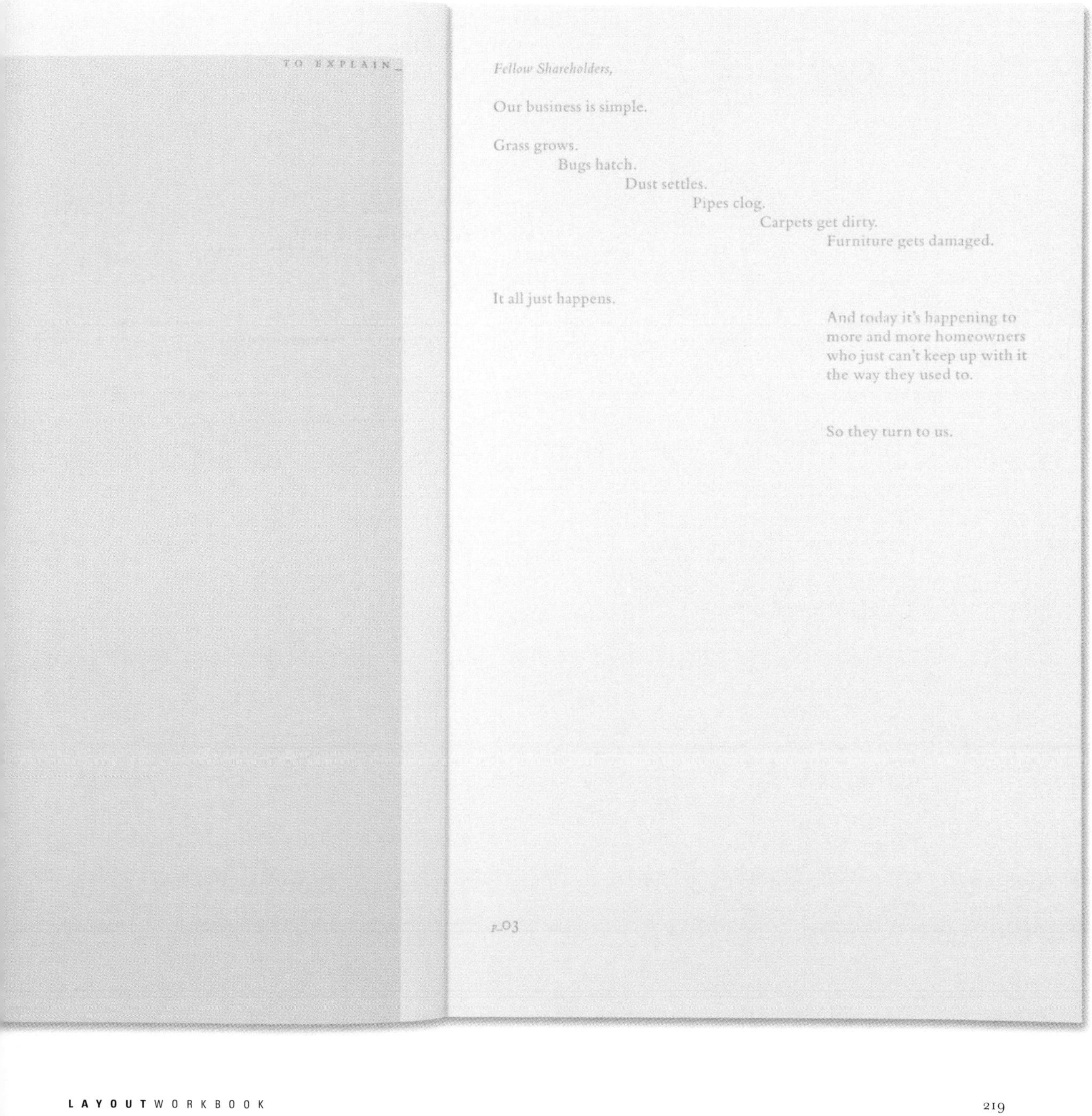

Fellow Shareholders,

Our business is simple.

Grass grows.
  Bugs hatch.
    Dust settles.
      Pipes clog.
        Carpets get dirty.
         Furniture gets damaged.

It all just happens.

      And today it's happening to
      more and more homeowners
      who just can't keep up with it
      the way they used to.

      So they turn to us.

p.03

Dividing the page into numerous spatial intervals accommodates typography that cascades across the page in flush left alignments. The movement is quick and brings visual activity to the page. Breaking the text into short, thoughtful pieces enhances readability.

Seyle: Words is flexibly composed, demonstrating changes in flush left, right, and centered alignments throughout the design. Bodies of text change position on each spread; some fall onto the left page, whereas others rest on the right. The writings are balanced by pale green rectangles that contain titles of each piece and move along the top edges toward the gutter. None of the writings have visual dominance—the pacing through the design is fluid. "Each piece was treated equally, so that one could easily pick up the book and read any selection," explains Kao. "However, from a writing standpoint, the pieces of work were selected and placed in a specific sequence to create a logical flow from start to finish."

SO WE TOOK WHAT WAS RIGHT ABOUT THE PLATFORM AND:

Shrank it to a fraction of its former size,
reduced energy requirements by 95%,
and made it price competitive...

Opened it to embrace industry standards,
both hardware and software...

Diversified it to support the products
of more than 1,000 vendors...

Networked it for easy, secure linkage
to other mainframes, to client/server systems,
to the Worldwide Web, to whatever you want...

Clustered it for transparent parallel processing
so if something goes down, it's not a problem;
if your transaction rates explode, it's no big deal;
if your data quintuples, you keep on ticking...

Automated it so work gets done in the proper order
without human intervention...

AND INTEGRATED EVERYTHING.

Two alignment points create the structure needed to integrate flush left paragraphs. The in-and-out motion separates the text into approachable pieces that are easily readable. The type size and leading is generous, which also increases readability. Small capitals are used on the first and last lines for distinction.

The sophisticated design of *Seyle: Words* illuminates the writing, which is the primary function of the piece. The content of the book drives the design; its presentation makes the initial connection to the viewer. "The subtle use of color and simple typography that we chose made the book appear calming to the senses. We wanted to make sure that we allowed enough attention to detail so the book appeared valuable and worth keeping," concludes Kao. "So far, the response has been successful in gaining new clients for the writer. The investment has already paid for itself."

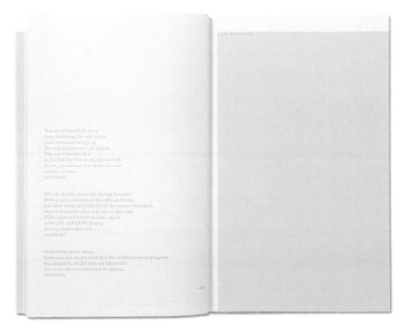

Typographic subtleties include the use of Bembo Italic, as well as small capitals, which are used in limited quantities to create emphasis. Italic and small capitals are visually distinct and provide a nice contrast to the roman font.

The use of capitals set in a centered alignment demonstrates progressive changes in type size, which create visual distinction between the lines of text and add typographic color to the page. The capitals are proficiently spaced, which is critical to this typographic setting.

SHINNOSKE INC.

art director, designer shinnoske sugisaki
creative director tomio sugaya

A design project that honors another designer is a difficult challenge. Should the design mirror the style of the subject or adopt a neutral personality? Although imitation is the highest form of flattery, it is not an inventive approach toward design, which is meaningless if it is a reproduction of existing aesthetics or trends. For all projects, visual solutions that accurately reflect content and function will best serve clients and viewers.

Shinnoske Inc. designed *Yoshio Hayakawa: His Design, Times and Osaka* to honor Hayakawa, a pioneer of Japanese graphic design. Art director/designer Shinnoske Sugisaki faithfully presents Hayakawa's work as "timeless design," he says. "I wanted to make this book have [the same] feelings as the original work." Its presentation is formal, allowing the work of Hayakawa to rise to the foreground without the distraction of competing visual elements. It is an informative solution that presents the content objectively, without bias. "Accurate information design makes true impressions to people," states Sugisaki.

Working directly with the client, the Osaka City Museum of Modern Art, Sugisaki explains his methodology: "When I got this project, I first discussed [production] with the curator—the number of pages, size, binding, paper, and cover—because I thought that its concept could be found from [the] format of the book. The curator and I made a decision that the book should be created not to be a record of old work but to be an excellent, fresh book, especially for young designers and students." The project developed when Sugisaki examined the work of Hayakawa to gain an understanding of its scope. "I looked through all the work of Hayakawa," describes Sugisaka. "All his designs were made on paper, not electronic material, of course. I found by touch that a kind of aura comes from such old materials. So, I took some elements for [the] design motif of the book, [including] some graphic elements for printing systems, such as trim and crop marks, which had been seen on finished work before [the] age of desktop publishing." The research phase enhanced the concept and directly informed the final design. Though the presentation of Hayakawa's work is traditional, the crop and trim marks are subtly applied throughout the design to add modernity, bringing the design into the present.

早川良雄の時代――― デザイン都市・大阪の軌跡

One of the remarkable features of Yoshio Hayakawa's design work is the use of color. The cover reflects this characteristic by combining transparent layers of hues that commingle to enhance the impression. Applied on a field of white, the effect is soft and poetic.

Yoshio Hayakawa: His Design, Times and Osaka is simply formatted to allow the work of Hayakawa to be respectfully featured. Each piece is composed in the center of the page to exalt its presentation. The alternating scheme of colorful backgrounds adds variety without interference. The viewer enters the design with ease. Shinnoske Inc. captures the essence of Yoshio Hayakawa in a straightforward, thoughtful design.

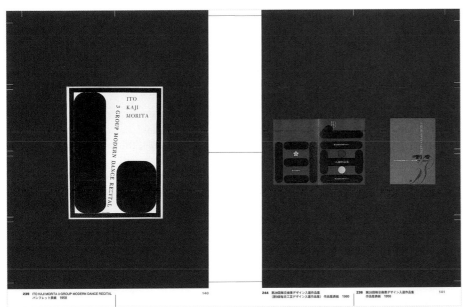

The work of Hayakawa dominates the interior spreads, which are characterized by a flexible structure. The layout of each spread varies and is based on the size of Hayakawa's work and how each piece complements the shape of the page. Typography supports the imagery, quietly residing on the bottom of the spreads as minimal, descriptive text.

Expansive backgrounds of color provide the surface areas that contain Hayakawa's work. Connoting his distinctive use of color, the hue variations add interest and enliven the presentation. Thin lines (intentionally applied crop and trim marks) connect the spreads horizontally and add aesthetic details along the edges of the pages, giving it a more contemporary feel.

STUDIO NAJBRT

designer ales najbrt

Daily Companion, designed by Studio Najbrt, is a newspaper that accompanies an exhibition at the Municipal House in Prague. The newspaper and exhibition feature contemporary Czech design (industrial, graphic, furniture, glass, pottery, china, and textile design). The goal of *Daily Companion* is to "introduce good-quality design available for everyone, not just for wealthier clients," explains designer Ales Najbrt. The design demands a utilitarian approach to reach the intended masses. Newspapers connote the everyday; they are affordable and readily available. Newspapers also provide quick, accessible information. *Daily Companion* is an overview of Czech design in a format that is straightforward and disposable. The newspaper "was a new and exciting experience for us," states Najbrt.

The inspiration for *Daily Companion* is "the lifestyle of young people who live simply and cheaply," explains Najbrt. "Quality does not have to be expensive." To reach the target audience, the aesthetic is bold and contemporary. "Black-and-white photography [is used], which is contradictory to a presentation of top design as we know it," discusses Najbrt. Photography, typography, and a black, red, and blue color palette interact. The visual elements are distributed evenly across and down the strict, columnar pages.

The front page of Daily Companion *is an integration of unusual photography and simple typography. The title sits boldly on top of the image. Subordinate typographic information, set in Helvetica Neue CE, provides information about the exhibition. This text enables flow around the composition and highlights the playful characteristics of the photograph.*

Quality

DOES NOT

have to be **expensive***.*

The typographic treatment of *Daily Companion* is characterized by large, red letterforms that rise to the foreground of the composition. They are dynamic indexes that lead the viewer into specific sections of the newspaper. Though the letterforms dominate, covering the photographs and text, they are decisively transparent. The design is readable without sacrificing impact. In addition, color is applied to the body text to separate information into usable segments. Black text represents the Czech language, whereas blue marks English. The bilingual presentation increases the functionality of the design.

The practicality of *Daily Companion* shifts the perception of design and makes it accessible to the public. By using a medium that is approachable and recognizable, the design challenges the stereotypical image that design is reserved for the elite. As the title of the newspaper suggests, design is for everyone on a daily basis.

Oversized letterforms, set in AG Book Stencil, are applied throughout the design as visual pointers. For example, G indicates the location of graphic design, whereas T leads the eye toward textile design. It is a hierarchically forward approach that provides emphasis and breaks the monotonous rhythm of the long columns of text.

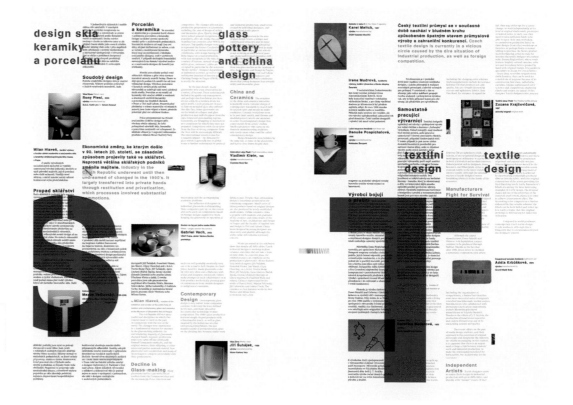

PRO KAŽDÝ DEN OUR DAILY COM PANION

Igor Němec,

radní hlavního města Prahy

Jsem velice rád, že mohu představit výstavní projekt s mottem Design pro každý den, který širokou veřejnost seznamuje s estetikou předmětů každodenní potřeby. Tento projekt, který se koná pod záštitou hlavního města Prahy, je výrazným obohacením kulturní našeho města a představuje umění, které se každodenně objevuje ve výstavních síních, ale o to více ovlivňuje estetiku našeho života.

Výstavní projekt je koncipován neobvyklým způsobem. Oproti tradičnímu pojetí v podobě expozitů z muzeí a galerií se jedná o podobu velké souvislé vnitřní soustředí s historickou nádherou interiérů Obecního domu, jehož národní rekonstrukce se stala ozdobou pražského památkového fondu a dokumentuje péči hlavního města o dědictví minulosti.

Dovolte mi popřát tomuto výstavnímu projektu následný úspěch u návštěvníků.

Navštivte, zhlédněte, čtěte

Dagmar Vernerová,

ředitelství společnosti Prostor

Já jsem přesvědčena, jak problematické je to arrive at a jednoduchou a srozumitelnou definici pojmu design.

Dagmar Vernerová,

Prostor, non-profit organization

It is almost surprising how difficult it is to arrive at a simple and comprehensible definition of the term "design" — a word that we use intuitively and that we encounter every single day in its materialized form, although sometimes not quite consciously.

Igor Němec,

councillor of the Capital City of Prague

I am very pleased to be able to introduce an exhibition project with the motto Everyday Design that introduces the general public to the aesthetics of objects of everyday use. This project taking place under the auspices of the Capital City of Prague significantly enriches our city's culture and represents art that may seldom appear in exhibition halls but perhaps even more so has a great impact on the aesthetics of our lives.

This exhibition project is conceived in an unusual way. Unlike the traditional presentation of museums and gallery exhibits, this exhibition is designed to resemble a large contemporary showroom harmoniously laid out in the historical splendor of the interiors of the Municipal House, whose sophisticated renovation is one of the gems among Prague's monuments and which testifies to the care dedicated by the capital city to its heritage.

Jana Pauly,

kurátorka výstavy

Zdeněk Zdařil,

spolupráce in collaboration with

Zdeněk Mrkvica, 1996

prototyp

Vladimír Rendl,

výroba manufactured by

Jiří Španihel, 2001–2002

výroba manufactured by

Ivan Dlabač, 1999

výroba manufactured by

Alexius Appl, 2002

výroba manufactured by

OEZ Letohrad

Vývojové trendy průmyslového designu v Evropě nebyly ve druhé polovině 20. století nikdy určovány československými designéry a výjimku netvořila ani léta devadesátá. Naopak se radikální změna politického systému a následných ekonomických poměrů odrazila negativně především v činnosti designérů působících ve strojírenství.

Czechoslovak designers never set development trends in industrial design in the second half of the 20th century in Europe; the 1990's were no exception to this rule. On the contrary, the radical change of political system and the ensuing economic changes had a negative impact in particular on the activities of designers working in the engineering industry.

Začalo se od nuly

průmyslový design

Někteří se už prosadili

Generační obměna

Some ...

Changing ...

Start from Scratch

industrial design

by Jana Pauly, curator of the exhibition and head of the industrial design department of the National Technical Museum in Prague

SUPERBÜRO

designer barbara ehrbar

700 documents the conception, development, and completion of the Pavilion Art Place in Magglingen, Switzerland. The pavilion, designed by :mlzd architects for an annual exposition, was constructed of seven hundred plastic storage boxes. (The temporary building was used as an artists' workshop during the exposition.) Superbüro was approached by :mlzd architects to design an accompanying booklet to celebrate the innovative structure. "The booklet is basically a souvenir of the pavilion and functions like a set of postcards that wake the memories," explains designer Barbara Ehrbar.

The primary goal of *700* was to create "a small, compact, easily sellable and producible publication." Unfortunately, the design needed to be completed within one week (and with a limited budget), which truncated the process considerably. "There was not much time for big concepts," adds Ehrbar. Although there was no sketching involved, there was "a lot of research and talking to architects and trying to understand the concept of the building," notes Ehrbar. Information-gathering, which included collecting and organizing large amounts of imagery and text, accounted for much of the design process.

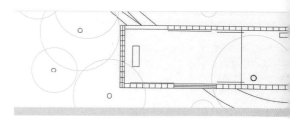

The cover of *700*, composed of seven hundred rectangles (the same number of plastic storage boxes were used to build the Pavilion Art Place), is light and airy. The gridded presentation is combined with one typographic element, *700*, in the bottom-right corner. The cover is sparse, the lack of information compelling.

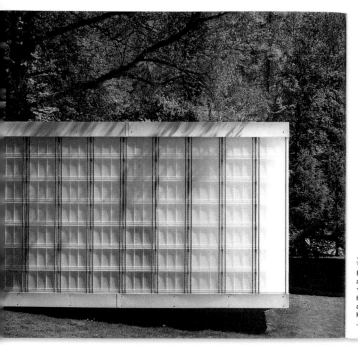

VERGÄNGLICHE HÜLLE FÜR EIN BEFRISTETES DASEIN Es ist nicht übertrieben zu behaupten, dass die Eidgenössische Turn- und Sportschule in Magglingen zu den besten architektonischen Zeugen zählt, die die Erinnerung an die Landesausstellung von 1939 in Zürich wachrufen. Zwar hatte die berühmte Landi ihre Tore schon geschlossen, als 1941 die ersten Vorprojekte für die Sportanlage in Angriff genommen wurden und einige Jahre werden noch verstreichen bis zum endgültigen Entwurf und dessen Ausführung im Jahre 1947. Doch alles, sowohl was die architektonische wie auch die landschaftliche Gestaltung der Bauten betrifft, bekundet dieses sensible Gleichgewicht zwischen Heimatgebundenheit und Moderne, das die Zürcher Landesausstellung erfolgreich hatte unter Beweis stellen wollen.

003

Ein allgegenwärtiges Thema der Expo.02 ist die schwebende Plattform, die aus der Höhe ihrer Pfähle die unwahrscheinlichsten Baugründe heimisch heraustordert. Es wäre nicht genug, in dieser Art die Bauten vom Boden loszulösen, allein die Umsetzung eines der Grundprinzipien moderner Architektur zu stellen. Je mehr man sich von lokalen Bedingungen des Geländes loslöst, gemeinhin lässt sich die Idee der rationalen Vollkommenheit erreichen. Was bei Expo.02 auf dem Spiel steht, ist etwas Anderes: es geht darum, die Orte vorübergehend fast unmerkst auszunützen, ohne Spuren zu hinterlassen. Gleichzeitig und paradoxerweise geht die Verminderung der Stützpunkte auf dem Boden mit der Suche nach einem engen Kontakt mit den Naturelementen einher: fussiof streicheln die Plattformen das Wasser, spielerisch ragen die Strukturen in den Himmel und beziehen die Wolken, liebevoll werden die Bäume in die Architektur eingeschlossen samt den Licht- und Schattenspielen ihrer Blätter. Unter diesem Gesichtspunkt und trotz einer teilweisen Bejahung gewisser Themen der Moderne hatten damals die Architektur der Landi und diejenige, die später von ihr beeinflusst wurde, die Werte der Verwurzelung und einer im wörtlichen Sinne verstandenen Bodenständigkeit nie ganz aufgegeben.

PAVILLON ZWISCHEN DEN BÄUMEN **DIE POETISCHE PARALLELAKTION MIT NAMEN «ARTPLACE» IST HOCH ÜBER BIEL IM GRÜNEN, AN DER END-DER-WELTSTRASSE NEBEN DER ALTEN SPORT- HALLE DER EIDGENÖSSISCHEN SPORTSCHULE MAGGLINGEN REALISIERT WORDEN. «ARTPLACE» BEHERBERGT BIS ZUM 19. OKTOBER 2002 ÜBER 20 KUNSTSCHAFFENDE, DIE ABWECHSELND IN ZWEIERBESETZUNG ZUM THEMA «BEWEGUNG UND SPORT» ARBEITEN. DER ELEGANTE PAVILLON KAM AUF EINER WIESE MIT BÄUMEN ZU STEHEN. SEIN OFFENER INNENHOF INTEGRIERT EINE BUCHE SOWIE EINE BRONZEPLASTIK.**

The interior of 700 flows horizontally, with each spread spilling over to the next. Typography spans the length of the page, connoting the shape of the pavilion. Spatially composed along the edges of the page, the type objectively informs and relies on the photography to tell the full story.

Inspired by the building, as well as its architects, Superbüro designed the format of *700* based on the proportions of the pavilion. Relying heavily on photography to explain the narrative, typographic content is limited. Its use, like the size of the booklet, is visually connected to the rectangular shape of the building. "The outline type emphasizes the light, open structure of the building," discusses Ehrbar. "The text stretched over the whole page is a synonym for the long shape of the pavilion." The typography works with the active, communicative photography and graphic shapes. However, it is generally isolated near the bottom or top of the pages as a secondary or tertiary element.

Color, graphic shape, photography, and typography unite to record a unique, architectural experience. *700* adheres to architect Louis Sullivan's dictum, "Form follows function." The design decisions honor the content from the format to the layout. "Functionality in design is important," expands Ehrbar. "But function alone is mostly boring. In my view, the right combination of functionality and 'sex appeal' is what makes good design."

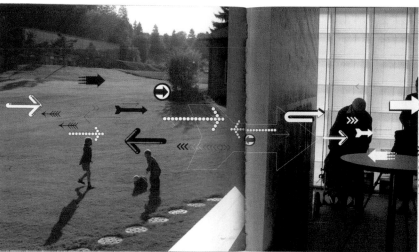

FLIESSENDER RAUM,
GROSSE FLÜGELTÜREN
SOWIE SCHIEBEWÄNDE
ERMÖGLICHEN EINE
MOBILE RAUMAUFTEI-
LUNG DES "ARTPLACE".
DIE TRANSLUZENTEN
KUNSTSTOFFBEHÄLTER
KOMMUNIZIEREN EIN
FARBLICHES WECHSEL-
SPIEL DER ÄUSSEREN
LICHTVERHÄLTNISSE INS
INNERE, WAS NEBEN DEM
JEWEILIGEN SONNEN-
STAND VOM SCHATTEN
DER BEWÖLKUNG ODER
DEM GRÜN VON IM WIND
SCHAUKELNDEN ÄSTEN
BEEINFLUSST WIRD.

Die flexible Ausstattung des Pavillons gestattet es, sowohl den Bedürfnissen einzelner Kunstschaffenden nachzukommen, die hier im Turnus einige Tage schöpferischer Zurückgezogenheit geniessen dürfen, wie auch den Anforderungen punktueller festlicher Anlässe zu entsprechen. Diese Alternanz von verschiedenen Nutzungen im gleichen Raum ist besonders klug. Sie verdeutlicht nämlich die für die Reifung und den Austausch von kulturellen Werten notwendige Wechselwirkung von Rückzugs- und Begegnungsmöglichkeiten, von Zeiten der Ruhe und reger Geselligkeit, von Orten der Besinnung in unmittelbarer Nähe der Naturelemente und Orten der feierlichen Anerkennung jener schöpferischen Leistungen, die eine dynamische Gesellschaft in sich zu wecken vermag. Artplace macht all dies möglich, und zwar mit bescheidenen Mitteln. Dieser Kunstgriff freut insbesondere diejenigen, die hinter die Kulissen schauen. Wer auch immer hierher kommt, stellt fest, dass er hier nur vorübergehend zu Gast ist, dass andere zeitweilige Präsenzen ihm vorausgegangen sind und ihm mit anderen Vorhaben folgen werden. Der Raum ist für die unerwartetsten Nutzungen frei, unter der einzigen Bedingung, dass das, was entliehen wurde, auch wieder zurückgegeben wird. Die Mehrzweckkiste aus Kunststoff, die dem modularen Grundstein des Pavillons ausmacht, ist ein Symbol für sich: aufgestapelt und mit Spannbändern befestigt definiert sie einen Ort des Verweilens; für den normalen Gebrauch wieder freigegeben wird die Kiste zu einem Transportmittel, das von Hand zu Hand weitergereicht wird.

020/021

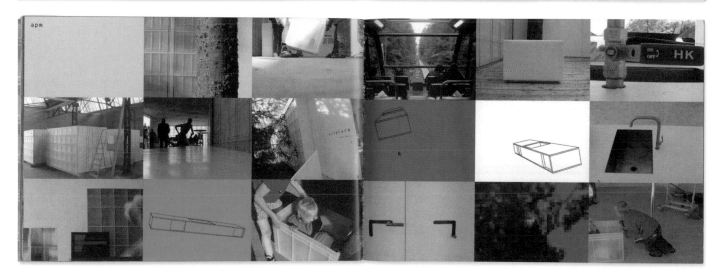

Additional interior spreads narrate the materialization of the pavilion from beginning to end. Color photographs are given full priority. Handled in numerous ways, imagery fills the pages. Images are contained in circles and rectangles and silhouetted in space. Layered with graphic shapes, such as lines and arrows, the photographic sequence comes alive.

WILSONHARVEY/LOEWY

designer paul burgess

The James Martin Institute for Science and Civilization can be described by the phrase Shaping the Future. Excerpted from their mission statement: "The James Martin Institute for Science and Civilization will identify science and technology issues critical in shaping the future of world civilization. It will conduct research to help humanity to shape a brighter future for itself and the natural environment on which it depends." WilsonHarvey/Loewy approached the design of the James Martin Institute brochure with the purpose of "attracting funding for the world's most leading-edge think tank, as well as to convey a sense of the future and mankind's gradual path toward self-destruction," explains designer Paul Burgess. "[The brochure] shows the [investors] and potential researchers where the studies may lead."

The inspiration and conceptual direction for the brochure "came from the studies [and] underlying issues currently facing us: global warming, nanotechnology, cloning, and corporate abuse," adds Burgess. The minimal design is inviting; the quantity of textual and visual information is succinct and visually dynamic. "We used space as our greatest asset. The whiteness of the pages gives a clinical, scientific feel, whereas the graphic devices add a technological slant," says Burgess. Short, narrow columns of black typography move along the top and bottom of the spreads. They are readable and allow the viewer to easily digest information. Blue textual elements slightly larger in size and shorter in length than the black type move freely around the compositional space calling attention to key points. Burgess elaborates, "You can connect with the blue type and read the brochure on one level, or the black type and read it in more depth. This is a classic case of using the information to lead the visual, and it's been extremely successful."

The use of space is the key element of the brochure. The openness of the design is evident on the cover, which introduces the dominant visual elements: clean, minimal typography and photography, and lines and graphic shapes that lead the eye through the composition and define the edges of the page.

In addition to the typography, the white space draws attention toward full-color photography, which is also quietly composed. "The use of space was always the basis of the brochure, and consequently, we had room to work visually interesting page dynamics around that space," says Burgess. Delicate linear elements, as well as graphic shapes and plus signs, enhance the visual field and connote precision, science, and technology. "The space, color, and graphics allow the eye to be thrown around the page in different ways," notes Burgess.

The subtlety and spaciousness of the James Martin Institute for Science and Civilization brochure draws immediate attention. It communicates efficiently with aesthetic strength. White space activates the positive areas of the design and leads the eye directly to the visual and typographic content. "We were very experimental, and luckily, the client loved our exploratory routes. The greatest challenge is always the communication of information: By letting the information do the work, the result is always very satisfying," concludes Burgess. "£10 million of funding was secured for the project once the brochure was produced."

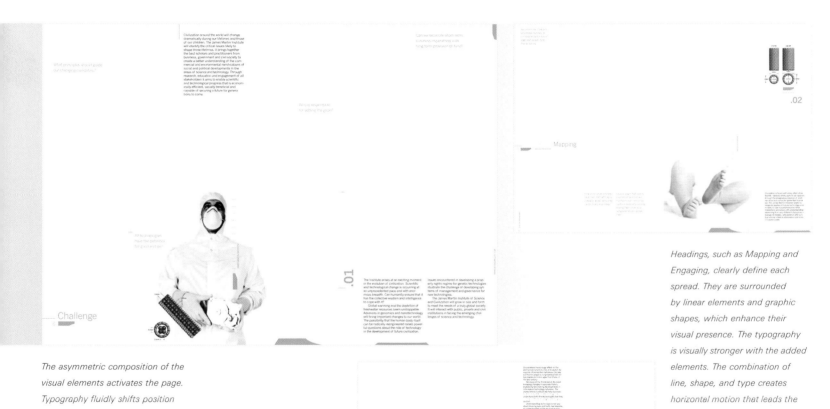

The asymmetric composition of the visual elements activates the page. Typography fluidly shifts position on each spread. Numbers are used to note sections (they are also the largest typographic element), and sans serif columns of body copy are composed along the top and bottom margins. The type size, column width, and length facilitate readability.

Headings, such as Mapping and Engaging, clearly define each spread. They are surrounded by linear elements and graphic shapes, which enhance their visual presence. The typography is visually stronger with the added elements. The combination of line, shape, and type creates horizontal motion that leads the viewer into the compositions.

alignment *The horizontal and vertical positioning of visual elements within the compositional space. It also refers to paragraph settings, including flush left, flush right, centered, and justified.*

ascender *The stroke of a lowercase letter that rises above the meanline.*

baseline *The horizontal line on which letters sit.*

cap height *The height of the capital letters measured from the baseline to capline.*

capline *The horizontal line along the top of the uppercase letters.*

centered *A paragraph setting in which text is ragged along the right and left edges.*

character *A mark, symbol, or sign, including letterforms and numbers, in language systems.*

color *In typographic terms, color refers to the density of typographic elements and their perceived gray value. It is the overall feeling of lightness and darkness on the page.*

column *A vertical division of space on a grid that is used to align the visual elements.*

column interval *An inactive, negative space, also known as gutter width, which separates one column from the next and prevents textual and visual elements from colliding.*

counter *The white space located inside of and around letterforms that affects legibility, readability, and density of typefaces.*

descender *The stroke of a lowercase letter that falls below the baseline.*

em dash *A punctuation mark used to separate thoughts within a text. There are no spaces needed before and after, but kerning may be required.*

en dash *A punctuation mark used in compound words and to separate items such as dates, locations, times, and phone numbers. The en dash can also be used to separate thoughts within a text. When an en dash is used in this manner, spaces are added before and after the dash.*

figure-ground *The relationship of visual elements within the compositional space that defines the positive and negative areas of the design. The ground, or negative space, defines the positive space, or figure.*

flowline *A horizontal measure that divides the page into spatial divisions and creates additional alignment points for the placement of the visual elements.*

flush left, ragged right (fl/rr) *A paragraph setting in which text is evenly aligned along the left edge, whereas the right edge of the text is ragged.*

flush right, ragged left (fr/rl) *A paragraph setting in which text is evenly aligned along the right edge, whereas the left edge of the text is ragged.*

folio *Page number.*

font *A set of characters from a specific typeface in one size, style, weight, and width.*

grid *A series of intersecting axes that creates horizontal and vertical spatial divisions.*

grid module *An active spatial field on a grid that accommodates the placement of visual elements.*

indent *A spatial interval used to signal a change from the paragraph preceding it.*

justified (fl&r) *A paragraph setting in which text is evenly aligned along the right and left edges.*

kerning *The typographic technique, also known as letterspacing, used to adjust (open and tighten) the slight distances between letters to avoid character collisions, as well as irregular and unwanted spaces.*

leading *The space between lines of text that is measured from one baseline to the next; it is expressed in points.*

legibility *The recognition of individual letterforms and their relative position to other letterforms in word formation.*

letterspace *The space between letters.*

ligature *A specially designed character produced by combining two or three letters into one unified form.*

line length *The length of a line of type; it is expressed in picas.*

lining figure *A number that shares the same height and width as full capitals.*

margin *The typically inactive spatial area on a grid that defines the active area of the compositional space and directs the viewer toward the visual elements.*

negative leading *The space between lines of text measured from one baseline to the next when it is decreased to a size less than the type size used. For example, 8 point type set on 6 point leading; it is expressed in points.*

non-lining figure *A number that shares the same x-height as lowercase letters and feature ascenders, descenders, and variable widths. Also known as an old style figure.*

orphan *One or two words from the previous spread that start on a new page, which should be corrected to avoid drawing attention to the isolated elements.*

pica (p) *A unit of measure that expresses line length and column width. 1 pica equals 12 points; 6 picas equal 1 inch.*

point (pt) *A unit of measure that expresses type size and leading. 72 points equals 1 inch; 12 points equals 1 pica.*

prime marks *Punctuation marks (' ") that denote feet and inches, not apostrophes and quotation marks.*

recto *The right page in publication design.*

readability *The recognition of how typography is presented as words, lines, and paragraphs. It is influenced by the typographic arrangement, including such factors as line length, leading, and spacing.*

rivers *A series of inconsistent word spaces that creates distracting open lines running vertically through the justified paragraph.*

sans serif *A typeface without serifs.*

serif *A finishing stroke added to the main stems of letterforms.*

small capitals *A complete set of uppercase letters that are the same height as lowercase letters.*

style *In typographic terms, the style of a typeface indicates if it is regular (also roman), italic (also oblique), or bold.*

tracking *The typographic technique used to adjust (open and tighten) the overall spacing of words, lines, and paragraphs to improve the readable appearance of text.*

typeface *The specific design of a full character set (alphabet, numerals, punctuation, diacritics) that is unified by consistent visual properties.*

verso *The left page in publication design.*

weight *In typographic terms, weight refers to the lightness or darkness of letterforms marked by a change in stroke width. It is indicated by terms such as light, medium, bold, heavy, and black.*

width *In typographic terms, width refers to different variations within a typeface family, such as condensed, compressed, or extended fonts.*

widow *One or two words that are left over at the end of the paragraph, which should be corrected to avoid drawing attention to the extra space.*

word space *The space between words.*

x-height *The height of the lowercase letters without ascenders and descenders.*

Baines, Phil and Andrew Halsam. *Type and Typography.*
New York: Watson-Guptill Publications, 2002.

Bringhurst, Robert. *The Elements of Typographic Style.*
Canada: Hartley & Marks, 1997.

Carter, Rob, Ben Day, and Philip Meggs.
Typographic Design: Form and Communication.
New York: Van Nostrand Reinhold, 1985.

Craig, James and William Bevington. *Designing
with Type: A Basic Course in Typography.* New York:
Watson-Guptill Publications, Fourth Edition, 1999.

Elam, Kimberly. *Expressive Typography: The Word
as Image.* New York: Van Nostrand Reinhold, 1991.

Ginger, E.M. and Erik Spiekermann. *Stop Stealing
Sheep & Find Out How Type Works.* California:
Adobe Press, 1993.

Hurlburt, Allen. *The Grid: A Modular System
for the Design and Production of Newspapers,
Magazines, and Books.* New York:
Van Nostrand Reinhold Company, 1978.

Hurlburt, Allen. *Layout: The Design of the Printed Page.*
New York: Watson-Guptill Publications, 1977.

McLean, Rauri, ed. *Typographers on Type.*
New York: W.W. Norton & Company, 1995.

Müller-Brockman, Josef. *Grid Systems in Graphic Design.*
Switzerland: Arthur Niggli Ltd., Switzerland, *1981.*

Rand, Paul. *A Designer's Art.*
New Haven: Yale University Press, 1985.

Rand, Paul. *Design, Form, and Chaos.*
New Haven: Yale University Press, 1993.

Samara, Timothy. *Making and Breaking the Grid:
A Graphic Design Layout Workshop.*
Massachusetts: Rockport Publishers, 2003.

Process: A Tomato Project.
California: Gingko Press, 1997.

ABOUT THE AUTHOR

ACKNOWLEDGMENTS

thank you

for friendship, guidance, humor, support, and wisdom

rockport publishers
kristin ellison
betsy gammons
regina grenier
all the contributing designers
my former professors at the university of illinois and risd
my colleagues at the university of cincinnati
my students
my friends
my family
booby, clem, and all the ladies
thom wakeman and craig ritter
margaret and steve
alex
dickie, K, and hoyt
deke haglahay (dune)
purp
the fabulous meghan eplett
dave extra thanks, bf

Kristin Cullen is a graphic designer and professor at the University of Cincinnati. She received a bachelor of fine arts in graphic design from the University of Illinois at Urbana–Champaign and a master of fine arts in graphic design from the Rhode Island School of Design. In her professional practice, including several years at Chicago firms, she has designed a wide range of communication materials. Her professional and academic work has been featured in exhibitions and publications, including Graphis, I.D., and Print.